VAGREIN

SEEKING ENDS WHEN SHARING BEGINS

CHANNELED BY JP HERMAN

You may contact us at www.jpherman.com

Cover & book design by JP Herman

ISBN: 979-85-5365-204-3

Original copies published and printed in November of 2020.
This is the September 2022 Version with some further editing and modification

TABLE OF CONTENTS

his book would not be in your hands right now if not for the amazing work and support from many people on my journey. I would like to take the time to thank them officially as I am ever grateful for all that they've done for me and Vagrein.

Over the many months of channeling Vagrein and putting together the content for this book, my family have constantly supported me, in every way, while showing me the true meaning of unconditional love in relationships. They are the reason why I have come to this Earth and every moment I spend with them is a blessing. I believe that without them in my life Vagrein would not have chosen to come through in the way that they have.

I am ever grateful for those special friends who have consistently been there for me with complete acceptance. Without the freedom you have allowed me to be my true self, channeling would not be possible and this book would not exist.

My collaboration with Gail Holwell has been enriching in so many ways. She selflessly poured through all the content with me, categorizing every paragraph in order, which has made the book infinitely more readable. Her attention to detail, commitment to the project and support have been invaluable. I could not have created this book without her.

Vagrein's work would have never reached public ears if not for the curiosity and enthusiasm of Karissa Wieskamp and Elisa Blaire. In embracing Vagrein and my fledgling channeling abilities in those very early days they showed me that the messages coming through were not meant only for me to hear, but to share with the world.

Special thanks goes out to all those who volunteered their time and energy in transcribing the many hours of audio sessions which make up the bulk of this book.

I am equally grateful for all of the participants in the public and private Vagrein sessions. Your questions provided Vagrein with opportunities to talk on subjects that are truly relevant and are of benefit to the whole collective at this time.

I would also like to acknowledge my spiritual teacher Bentinho Massaro for his example of alignment, his massive body of work on self-realization and the personal lessons that I learnt through interaction with him as a teacher.

Of course, a channeled book wouldn't be if not for the entity that was authoring it...

I am filled with immense love and grat-

ACKNOWLEDGMENTS

itude for Vagrein themselves for having chosen me for the amazing opportunity to channel their message.

Through my relationship with the group I have found my peace, my purpose and myself. Although they have always guided me on my path, working so closely in collaboration has been the most rewarding work and service I have experienced so far.

Lastly, and most importantly, I would like to thank you, the reader, who either through conscious choice or fate now hold this book in your hands. It would not have arrived to you in this moment without our destinies, and that of Vagrein, being infinitely intertwined. Thank you for the time and dedication required to absorb what you're about to read. May it enrich your life and the path you are on as it has entirely shifted my own.

With love and gratitude,
Jessie

It's the perfect illusion and challenge: To be thrust into a space that you call reality with such a profound level of forgetting of the simple understandings of **All-There-Is** in favor of the possibility of creating, with free will, a new light to shine into the infinity. A new version of everything; You. Welcome to being human.

There are no guidebooks, and yet a lot of books for sure; from your religious scriptures to your fiction to the beautiful drawings on cave walls or tree pulp. You're storytellers and you are telling yourselves the same stories over and over again. But you don't read between the lines. You're literal. Literately literal.

You hear words and forget that they are **vibrations** floating through the space of nothingness. You forget that they are marks on paper, some which absorb the light and some which do not. You are not able, as we are, to see or read past the words themselves and get the full transmission of the author or storyteller.

It is a limit, but one you can overcome. When you hear and see, listen and look for the energy between the words and the layers upon them, remember too that the authors themselves are often crippled by their own **beliefs**, in communicating freely and in sourcing the truth of their own stories.

It is wise to stop taking words so literally. Read through this text with your heart and ears as much as you do with your mind and your eyes and you will understand.

You may ask: "What is there to do?" There is nothing you must do.

Creation loves the fool and the wise man, and often they are one and the same. Creation loves the sinner and the saint, for they too are the same.

There can be no-one and no thing that is not, in its full being, everything all at the same time. There is no right and wrong. There is only Isness.

So why the instructions? Why the communication and the push towards waking the sleeping children?

Because you're ready. If you choose to be, you are ready. You're ready to let go of suffering completely. Ready to become pure freedom. Ready to remember what you have

WHERE TO BEGIN

known all along, that you came here for the sole purpose of choosing whether or not you preferred the light or the dark.

There are many of you now, fully mature and blossomed and ready to accept the responsibility of the choices that you have been making all along, but were unaware of. You're ready to become the creators, to choose instead of accepting a default.

There is enough faith now, enough clarity for you to stand up and say: "OK, this has taught me what I need to know but it's time to move on. Time to move forward. Time to become everything I want to be. Here, now, in this **incarnation**, with this reality, in this beauty." - *Vagrein, September 8th, 2016*

How to Use this Book

*The first thing you should know is that I am taking guidance on writing this book from a non-human, non-physical energy source. If you are unfamiliar with the concept of '**channeling**' luckily there is an entire section of this book dedicated to it. I believe that will lead to the most accurate representation of what wants to come through. This book has been written in collaboration with the non-physical entity group allowing themselves to be known as "Vagrein".*

Throughout the book you will be reading passages by myself, the author and channel, and those of the entity group. To distinguish between the two we have chosen to present the text that is written by myself in an italicized font and those of the entity group in regular characters.

The footnotes you will find in the book have also been added both by myself and the entity group and respect the same formatting.

At times you will come across words presented in bold text. These are either used for emphasis or described further at the end of the book in the glossary section.

Much of the content is derived from live channeling sessions occurring between July and December of 2019. The rest of the content has been channeled and written in 2020 or from earlier written transmissions that arrived between 2016 and 2018.

The book has been divided into themed chapters to make it easier for you to reference the wisdom on specific topics. Much of the content spans multiple topics, but I have endeavored to keep things as organized and simple as possible.

One suggestion is to read the text slower than you would read other informational volumes, with particular attention to the channeled elements.

Each word has been chosen by Vagrein in the specific order that they appear here in print and their way of conveying information is very clear even if the language at times is not one we are accustomed to. Often, they choose words that have double or triple meaning upon deeper examination and pondering. Allow yourself the time to soak in these multiple meanings in full.

*As channeled material is inherently non-verbal, and then translated via the human brain, I have found the entity group to be very creative in coming up with connections that we humans would not normally come up with, and even, at times, creating new words which convey concepts more fully than could have been done otherwise. Behind each word is also the corresponding energy transmission so again, go slow allow yourself the time to absorb what is written. If at any time you sense sleepiness or fogginess while reading, put down the book to absorb the information packet that is being delivered to you and pick it up again later. Vagrein has informed me that your action and **intention** to read this book is equivalent to consenting to completely and effortlessly integrate and embody the knowing within it.*

Please note that none of the information in this book is intended as gospel in any way. What has been offered and provided in this volume is the opportunity to choose what resonates for you and the possibility to apply it to your own life.

Vagrein has never claimed to be anything greater than human or above us in any way. Deification or idolization is not encouraged at all. Nor is the discussion, debate or reinterpretation of their words for any means other than personal understanding. What is being offered through this contact is not up for speculation or reading-into in order to determine its meaning.

In human history there have been countless incidents of pure information being confused and altered as one attempts to understand it, often to the detriment of the clear message beneath it. What one must remember while reading this work is that you are the ultimate authority, creator and chooser of your life experience. Adopt whatever understandings feel right for you, but do not give importance to their source.

What is transmitted here and what you choose to embrace will doubtlessly create connections for you relevant to your journey and therefore needs no further inter-pretation by the mind. You will know you have understood when you know you have understood.

As a channel, author and being walking alongside you on this planet for a time, my intention is to share what may or may not be serving you through the gifts that I have been granted. The ultimate discernment for how to use this information will then be up to you. Vagrein suggests the following methods for getting the most out of your reading experience:

There will be no way to get through the book you are about to read without some form of suspended belief. By this we ask you, for the duration of reading this text, to endeavor to hold off on applying what you think to be true in your mind, much like you would, should you be reading a work of fiction.

We do not ask you to believe what it is we are about to recount, but simply to feel into our words and this information in a very neutral and relaxed way. What is true for you will remain, what is not true for you will continue down the stream of **collective consciousness** and therefore it is of no consequence for you to hear it. There is never any need for **resistance** when one knows one's truth. This book will help point you in the direction of yours.

Our human co-author was under the impression and idea that it would be better for her to write this introduction and ease you into the knowing of the source of the materials you are about to read, however, we know that you are eager and ready to hear what we would say to you and any further delay is simply a form of manipulation that would be in place only to make you more comfortable.

There is nothing wrong with discomfort. It is the fertile soil of growth.

Herein we compile some of the information that we have shared with you, so far, in our verbal and written channeling sessions in a more digestible format: organized by category and functionality within one's life. The secondary scope of this particular work is to highlight the new form of relationship that is being made available to you as humans on this planet at this time. There is the potential for collaboration with beings that are non-physical, such as We, through the act of intending and allowing this type of relationship. We are asking the vessel/your narrator to write part of the book from her perspective; showing her experiences in the form story of how our relationship with her came to be and continues to be.

There will be those of you who are reading this work who choose upon completion to allow their own communication to begin with higher levels of **consciousness**. This choice will guide you to a place of understanding Self so as to be able to be one's self in service to all; to be what you came here to be.

Up until now most channeled work has been delivered in a very formal format with the information being treated as sterile.

We have noticed during our sessions with you that there is still some form of discomfort when talking with us. We understand that it is due, in part, to the delivery of the words, the lack of inflection or the lack of eye contact. We are currently working to improve our 'personability'[1]. There are also slight differences in our use of your language to which you are not accustomed.

Not all of the information that we are transmitting is being translated in your language. Much of what we have sent in the past is non-verbal or telepathic and you may, in your waking state, access it by releasing the resistance you hold in order to not have access to this information.

Presently, our communication is the equivalent of your Morse Code system and as you evolve in your receptivity, so will the systems by which we can communicate. We continue to emphasize these points because of your continued doubt and it is our attempt to tranquilize and re-balance the perception that leads you into the emotional state of doubt. For this state is of a lower vibratory level and lengthens the process unnecessarily.

A stigma surrounds channeling and channeled material even amongst those of you who are open-minded. There is a confusion that through this format one is talking to something outside of, or higher than, their own state of consciousness. We are not outside of you. We are not higher than your consciousness. All is possible and all is available and all is on its way. All is You.

For many of you this is the first contact you will have with non-physical or 'extraterrestrial' examples of the use of consciousness in forms you deem 'intelligent'. All forms of this intelligence are likewise non-external from you.

Ultimately you will understand that there is no external intelligence. This vast nature and variety of your internal intelligence will reveal itself once your positioning of Self shifts to what you truly are. Humanity now shifts towards the many contacts with other forms of consciousness. It is already happening all around you and within you. As more of you become open to contact with other beings there will be more and more opportunities to have such contact and to understand the nature of the waltz you engage

---

1 *The entity group is referring to their presentation during live channeling sessions. In most, the transmission is delivered with my eyes closed, there are long pauses as they search my brain for appropriate vocabulary, there is very little movement or facial expressions and there is little to no change in vocal inflection. The result is an experience that does not seem to have the same warmth we are accustomed to in human interactions.*

with. All this will be directly related to your choice to have this contact -Your free will.

We are speaking first of channeling and telepathic communication in general, but in time, physical manifestations and new realities will appear for you. However, before you imagine spaceships landing in your front yard, know that those of you who are open and willing will not be exposed to such a sudden shock. You will have your first contacts with other forms of consciousness. We being one of them. You will understand what is about to happen before it happens and you will be prepared to be the ground-team for that reality, if and when you choose for it to be your reality. Then, when contact manifests in a more seemingly dramatic way, you will not be surprised or shocked but simply know you are ready and open for the new adventure in interacting with more of yourself.

These contacts will be conscious, unconscious or semi conscious and are occurring right now. The words you're reading are your current accepted form of First Contact. Know that there is more to come. Your contact is already underway and all of you are what you call 'channeling' in your own specific fashion. This is the First Contact.

Your understanding of unity and forgetting of separation is allowing for a thinning of your experiential atmosphere. It is only a belief in separation that forces other beings into physical form and onto spacecraft. Often these are concessions made for you to be able to accept the 'reality' of their presence and of which they themselves truly have no necessity for.

There will be those, if you choose for there to be, who are not as prepared for direct five sense experiences with what you now perceive of other consciousness. These beings will find themselves in a state of shock as more and more of humanity's potential future reality is revealed to you. Having prepared yourselves with previous non-physical contacts in this way will allow you to aid in their processing of the new phenomena. The propensity towards separation is still so strong in your primal psyche - the more untangled and forgotten this confusion becomes, the easier the passage will be.

You will be able to help them because you will know that All-is-One.

And now for introductions: We have been called 'Vagrein' through our own proposal of the word. It is not 'our name' anymore than your name is yours.

Remember that you did not choose your name. It was given to you by your parents for the convenience and ability to call you something other than 'infant, baby or child'. This was the only way they could separate you in the nursery from the other newborns in your Plexiglas cages. It is a human act to give a name. It is the first act of separation imposed upon you.

We are nameless and yet we understand your habit and need for this action and so we suggest 'Vagrein' symbolically in a visualization of letters to your narrator/our channel as she held a specific desire to be led to a new understanding that words spoken, could not have led her to. We will allow her to tell you the story herself:

Before I share the story behind the name Vagrein I'll back up a little bit to give you some context on how all of this began. It was my fortieth birthday. I was walking through my kitchen tidying up some dishes when I 'heard' the familiar knock on my consciousness - almost an invitation - to channel. I put 'heard' in quotes here because it's not the kind of hearing that is done with the ears, or any part of the physical body. I've never been able to explain it but this kind of hearing isn't processed by the nervous system at all, it's more of a knowing of hearing.

*I had only become aware of 'channeling' a few years earlier in 2016 when I stumbled upon some **Abraham Hicks** quotes on-line and then looked them up on YouTube. I watched as Esther Hicks spoke on stage in the plural tense. I assumed that the reason was that she was speaking on behalf of a company or group. The message resonated and so I didn't think much of it and continued to listen.*

When I finally got the book 'Ask and It is Given[1]' I was puzzled, and a little put-off by the explanation at the beginning of the book about her channeling a non-physical entity group and how she had come to do so.

A few months afterwards, during my morning meditations, I started to feel a pressure on both sides of my head, like large hands were

1   Hicks, J., Hicks, E., Ask and It Is Given: Learning to Manifest Your Desires (Hay House Inc., 2004)

MEETING THE ENTITY GROUP

cupped over my ears. It wasn't an unpleasant feeling, just unusual and I realized that if I relaxed into it, my head would start moving on its own. It was as if this sensation was moving it. Curious, I continued the meditation and tried not to focus on what was happening, but on the observer[2], until I observed that my head was being moved into unusual and exaggerated positions on my neck.

It scared the hell out of me.

I could resist it and stop myself from moving, but then was not able to go as deep into meditation. Since it began happening every time I meditated I eventually gave up meditation altogether, frightened by what was happening. I was either going crazy or something external to me was moving my head.

I was no stranger to the paranormal, esoteric or metaphysical, but we certainly weren't friends. As a child I saw ghosts, heard voices, had a collection of imaginary friends (who weren't so imaginary) and had been contacted/visited with aliens[3] on many occasions. It may seem like a hefty sentence to just throw out there, and I can say it now candidly, but I didn't acknowledge any of this openly at the time, even to myself. All of the odd happenings, hauntings, and encounters with dead relatives and friends had been filed in my psyche under 'imagination' and I rarely, if ever, opened up and talked about them. These new experiences of my head moving during meditation went in that same cabinet and I locked it with a key.

Some time later when I slowly returned to meditation and the unusual side effects recommenced, I was more prepared and accepting of the unseen and unknown. This time, whenever my head would start to move while meditating, I would either allow the movements to happen or silently address the energy moving me and ask it to please not interfere. This would stop the moving immediately.

I developed a relationship with this energy, curious about what it wanted and where it was leading, but disinterested in actually following it down that path. The energy, or entity, was always there as a presence but I didn't want to invite it into my reality and could send it off with a simple 'no'. There were a few times I sat and typed away for hours at the keyboard with the same energy guiding me, but I was full of so much insecurity and doubt. I felt unready. I felt unworthy.

I decided to focus on studying **self-realization** and **enlightenment** while carrying on normally with my everyday life and role as a young mother. I studied

---

2 In many forms of meditation practice one is requested to detach their focus from what is being observed in their experience and instead focus on the witness of what is being observed.

3 I have not yet spoken completely openly about my personal experiences with extra-terrestrial visitors. These experiences continue presently and eventually I hope to have the possibility of understanding completely and sharing more on this topic.

everything I could find on the topic, found amazing teachers and had several deep awakening experiences that have left me forever changed.

The Internet was a wonderful place to meet like-minded people and even though there still weren't too many with whom I would talk about my experiences, those who I felt comfortable sharing with at least believed I wasn't going crazy. I got to meet some of them in person and developed friendships for the first time with people who I didn't feel were judging this aspect of me. This allowed me to begin to stop judging it myself.

It took years of searching within to understand that all of the paranormal and esoteric experiences I had had were not just an active imagination. I really did have **extrasensory** *gifts.*

So, there I found myself the kitchen with this invitation[4] to channel not even knowing if I could or if I actually wanted to. All I knew was that I was turning forty that day and that I had spent forty years running away from a big part of me. I was more than tired. I was exhausted. I was having to say no to this energy more and more frequently. I couldn't hold up the fort and I couldn't remember why I had to.

I put down the dish, downloaded a voice recording app on my phone, lay on my bed and went into a meditation for the first time ever with the intention of a 'Yes' instead of a 'No'.

What follows is the transcript from that very first verbal contact:

We are available. You already know everything you need to know. You're already able to speak for us. We are present.

We cannot speak to all of you because all of you will not hear. We use those of you in form to speak for us, so that those that would not hear directly can choose to misinterpret. The term 'alienation' is perfect.

There is no need to fear for even the alienation that you face as a bridge or a messenger is perfectly placed to respect those who do not wish to hear. It is a protection. You may continue to share your, or our message - which is the same - and those who do not wish to hear may think that there is something wrong with you. That you have made it up or that you are mentally unwell.

A part of them knows. A part of them hears anyways. There's a natural,

---

4 *While the invitation to channel can sometimes be insistent I have always held the ability to choose whether or not I will participate. It has never been involuntary or without the ability to stop it at any time. I am not in any way 'out of control' or 'possessed' while channeling.*

instinctual fascination with the truth and those who do not wish to hear with their ears or their heads may still choose to hear with their hearts and in their perfect time rise.

We watch as you continue to play games. Even the game to save the world is a game. The rising does not happen through action. You are already risen. It is not a verb. The dark ones, those who are sleeping, those who are actively harming, they need your **love**. There are no villains. Judgment is judgment.

You will walk, you will see, you will see things that you cannot resolve. It is because they are unresolvable. There was never anything to resolve. The atrocities, the horrors, as you call them, only exist because you choose to continue to see them as separate. Separate from what? Separate from the Creator which is you. You look away. You look away from yourself. One cannot resolve what is unresolvable. You cannot fix what is not broken. You cannot change the changeless.

God is the What-Is. You are.

We come. We come because we too play games. There are so many levels and this game is simultaneous.

The question is: What do you want? Do you want to play the game of saving the world in the world that does not need to be saved? Or, do you want the What-Is? Do you want God?

Saving or saved? Saved from what? Presumably you're trying to save the world from something? From what? What could you possibly be trying to save it from? Or humanity? From itself. Humanity is both the victim and the perpetrator. So as you save it you punish it. As one is enlightened one is condemned. One is freed one is caged. And yet, you spread the word, you spread the word, you spread the word. You talk of waking people up to what is....

-Alarm sounds-

I had set an alarm because I had to run an errand. As it rang I was shocked back to reality. I couldn't believe all that time had gone by in a flash. I knew I was talking but I couldn't remember what was said. It was like the deepest meditation I had ever experienced, but even deeper.

I, the I Am of I, was just displaced... Gone.

I hit the play button to listen back and was excited, shocked, delighted and a little bit concerned to hear the slow, quiet voice talking in that manner. It was easier to decide that it was just me talking to myself in some sort of elaborate self-delusion.

Yup, I was going crazy... Finally.

It didn't stop me though, and in the next two weeks I recorded another handful of sessions, listened back to them and transcribed them, each time coming to the same conclusion. In retrospect I don't know why I kept going but I'm glad that I did.

On my computer I found I had kept some written sessions from years earlier. I am including them here because while they may seem personal I feel the energy is intended for all those who felt as I did and who are stepping into their roles in the way that I was:

There is a huge amount of gratitude, appreciation and love for you for your decision to fill this role.

You are able, through a series of physical and emotive variables and through a preconceived contract, to tap into the source of our energy. You have always known this and have until now not consciously decided to partake in the agreement. Do not feel guilty for this, for there is no time, and what is relevant is your participation in the Now.

You will not be understood and it will not matter because the understandings are not and cannot be immediate. This communication is not urgent for anyone but you. The words translated here are brought for you to be able to ease into this new role and begin to have faith in your abilities. There is no need to rush. We and you are not going anywhere and there is no possibility of error.

You will learn and allow more and more. You are learning now. In some time, of your perceived time, you will look back on today and tomorrow and yesterday and marvel at how far you have come. It is only relevant that you keep existing. If it moves you to sit, for now, at these keys and tap away then do so, but feel no obligation. It is not needed and the development is underway in whichever way you see fit to relate to it.

You are on the right path, as well. You are exposing yourself consistently to other people who have walked your path, other channels for other entities. What is happening is real as long as you say it is. If you choose to say it is not, then it is not. Look inside yourself, try on both opinions and choose which feels right to you via your reaction to it. That is your personal truth, and from your point of All-There-Is consciousness, that is the only reality. Choose this as you would choose all other things and you will not be disappointed with the outcome.

Disregard what others may say for they cannot be inside of you. You will not be able to explain with words the process of receiving this information. You may choose, as others have, to adopt the information as your own or funnel it away from your personality construct. Both choices are valid. Know however that both choices have their relating effects and those will need processing too. In the meantime, take the emotion of doubt and insecurity that you feel and learn from them what they are trying to teach you. Your confidence was accurate. No one can know, and even if it looks to someone on the outside as arrogance, they are teaching you. Do not let them teach you to be a sheep. Do not allow them to teach you not to shine. These states, the dull passive state of following the crowd are temporary comforts and in the end do not help you to avoid anything but a falsely perceived threat that was never there in the first place.

You are all you suspect yourself to be. You are the grand master of your universe. You are the god you know is housed inside of you. You do have your powers. You do have your gifts. You do have the choice and the capability and the possibility to use them. You can change the world into what you want to see it as. You can accomplish the great things that are in your heart. You are already on your way.

Chin up girl, you have a beautiful path ahead of you.

You child, are one of us.

You have had no faith. You have used your mind as a tool for blocking our message instead of translating it but you are now ready.

Rest. Stop. Don't try.

There is nothing to prove. You do not need to prove to us what we already know. We already know. We can see you and see your heart. We can see every beautiful facet of the love that you have come into this world to be. We can see the struggle that this caused you and the strength that you have developed while struggling, but the struggle is over. The ties are cut, the bondage is unstuck, you are free.

Now you will do what you came here for. You will shine the light and this message. You will reach those who still struggle. They will resonate with the words that you choose through no longer having a choice to not choose the right words.

There is relief from desires ahead. There is peace from your demons. There is a flow of a river so powerful that anything other than surrender to its current would surely cause you to drown, and there is a knowing of this.

Don't fear the visions that you see anymore - That beautiful world where beings do come together and express themselves with knowing and security is on the horizon. You do not need to fear wanting it. You do not need to fear knowing it's possible. The voices of those who would tell you it's not possible are getting louder - but your ears are adjusting now and those voices are further away than your own.

Trust yourself. Trust yourself. Know.

And this phase you're going through, you are handling it well. We know it's painful to stretch in this way. We know that you are fearful. We see there is nothing to fear at all. The beauty. The beauty. The joy. You are so powerful, so beautiful, so fresh, so safe, so new.

You will have more visits and become more aware of them. We will be able to load you with more incentives and give you more responsibility as this moves. Do not rush. It is good that you are focusing on strengthening the mental and physical faculties. Keep this up. You will need these upgraded systems.

Do nothing. Do nothing that you are not called to do.

Listen for us. We are talking but also allowing plenty of time to rest. There is no rush as there is no time.

Remember...

There is nowhere you have to be.

There is nothing you have to do.

There is no way that you have to act .

There is no way to make a mistake.

You are in service.

You are of service.

You cannot not be of service.

You are already whole and complete and full.

You do not need to move even one millimeter to shift this and you cannot shift it even if you were to move the whole planet.

This is complete. You are service.

Your worries are unfounded.

Go now... be in the present moment. Enjoy those little beings around you who are also in service and paramount to the mission. There will be more. You know this.

Rest now.

Joy, love, being

Anainai[5]

More personal messages from before I had much faith in my channeling include:

You're very wise, child.

And yet often a fool.

And perfectly innocent.

We are with you, always.

And we know you can hear us.

And we know you have the heart to share.

We see the work you have been doing. How you're softly and gently moving through fear, letting it go. We see that you see love that's on the other side of your fear and how you're beginning to trust it. Trust yourself and trust others. We see how you've put down your shields and you've put down your swords and we can support you with that. There is no attack and you are held in this in-between. Cradled. Like Moses in a basket floating in deep security towards a destiny that you as a baby could not yet know. And yet you know. You can feel the spark and the light inside of you. You have come far enough to have faith in the current. You've surrendered enough and seen how small you are and how any form of struggle is both futile and unnecessary. There's a golden light surrounding you now. A certainty. And soon your remaining allegiances and ties that bind you will be revealed to have never been there and you will see that you were never bound.

You can rest. Rest in this last part of the journey for the first chapter is coming to an end and all that you've learned and all that you gathered will be put to use as we turn the next page. Allow yourself to feel how much love you have for what you still believe is imperfect. See how you have been enjoying all the remaining victim-hood. And be grateful for what it has given you. Soon it will be gone. So rest now. Rest and gather your energy knowing that it is safe to rest and that when you are finished resting you will be energized and in perfect timing you'll be called upon. And you will be ready.

---

5   *'Anainai' is often used to end transmissions or as a salutation. It has not been defined.*

With all that encouragement I continued with the sessions. On July 8th, 2019 they told me:

Your Earth team is forming around you. Each of which will have their specific role. And there is no urgency to its formation.

They were right...

*I* traveled to the Netherlands for a few weeks over the summer to stay with some friends in a beautiful old monastery converted into a communal living space for people interested in spirituality. While there I met two women, Karissa Wieskamp and Elysia Blaire who, upon hearing about my channeling adventures, encouraged me to find out what would happen if I attempted to channel with other people present.

They suggested we set up a session that night and to try to converse with the entity in the same way that audiences interact with Abraham Hicks or **Bashar** *- asking questions and seeing what came through.*

This was only fifteen days after my first verbal encounter allowing the entity group to speak through me and I was still dealing with so many emotions around channeling. I was feeling extremely nervous, insecure,exposed and embarrassed. I didn't have a clue what I was doing and I wasn't pretending to, either. Still, somehow I managed to effortlessly go into the **channeling state.**

The session that follows is part of that first conversation. In Italics you will read the questions posed by the participants, with the entity group[1] responding in standard font case.

- What's your name? Or could you tell me where you're from?

- There is resistance.

- How might we relieve this resistance?

- There remains too much insecurity on the part of the one who is talking. And disbelief. And fear of error. And so that which we are transmitting gets absorbed by the consciousness and yet will not be spoken. Like when one of you does not want to commit to going to a party, and so you do not say yes or no, to leave options open. It is the same with where we are from too much intellect and arrogance on the part of this vehicle, but we are working on that in collaboration.

When I am channeling all of my physical senses are active but are used to perceive the content of the chan-

---

1 Later known as 'Vagrein'.

SEEKING ENDS WHEN SHARING BEGINS

neled material. Therefore I'm not really aware of the physical world that surrounds my body during the sessions. Sometimes the information comes in visual format, sometimes just experiential knowing. Most of the time my body is talking and interacting without me. The 'me' as I know my own individuated consciousness, is not at all involved in the conversation itself.

When the entity was asked its name, I was shown in my mind's eye the capital letters V-A-G-R-E-I-N but because of the amount of doubt present in me, the information was not passed onto the participants with verbal communication. In early sessions I would block out parts of the transmission through resistance. This is what they meant by 'that which we are transmitting' I've since learnt to trust Vagrein more.

The next day I went on the Internet to look up the word and see if it had any meaning or significance. There was surprisingly little associations with the name. Then, on a website which helps new parents to choose baby names I found the name Vagrein with no explanation but these words: "Seeking Ends When Sharing Begins". I suddenly understood that having reluctance to say the name that was shown to me was an initiation rite for me as a channel. They were communicating to me, in a way that I could no longer doubt, that the first part of my spiritual journey, my spiritual childhood, was over.

Since then more information has been collected that describes them further. The following section answers some common questions that have arisen in various sessions about the Vagrein entity group in general.

WHO OR WHAT IS VAGREIN?

We can be described as a group of beings beyond physical materialization with shared consciousness, that communicate with you, at this time, because of a request brought through you, this group and those reaching for communication of this nature.

We are known as 'Vagrein'. This is a name, as any other name associated with us only for the ability to differentiate ourselves from other and therefore is not truly a name with which we would associate ourselves. Because you are in a situation where names are necessary for you to understand differentiation, which is a part of separation and not applicable to us, we have conceded the possibility of being called by this name for convenience sake. In reality we are not separate from any other aspect of consciousness.

You may call us whatever you like. There are no corrections, there are no errors. We are pleased that your vessel figured out our ruse and she learned the lesson we have proposed to her in this game. As all are included, our name would be far too long to pronounce, to be sure to include everyone/everything and if, for convenience sake, calling us Vagrein would be pleasing we have no objections to your choices.

The being that you know as Jessica has allowed us to speak through her as a vessel. This is because she has a particular configuration in her genetic makeup that allows this to be possible and has had experiences in her lifetime that have led to the point in which it is possible for this to occur.

WHAT ARE YOUR INTENTIONS + THEMES IN COMMUNICATING?

Our intention is to assist with transition from Separation Consciousness, which is what you as a planet are experiencing at this time, to Unity Consciousness.

There are many ways to describe this transition, people talk of densities or dimensions. We will say it is a question of perspective of what is unified or separate. We intend to aid you in finding your own road, towards a balance between love and wisdom.

Some of our counsel is useful to navigate one's personal life, some of our counsel is useful to navigate one's **belief systems**, or one's thoughts. That is why, we meet with you in this way.

Our will is your will. You are the only one who can determine our intention/will, and yet our will includes all will, because all will is One. We sense the circular nature of this statement and yet from where we are, there is nothing but the circle.

You are teaching yourselves. We could not present ourselves in your reality without your intention for us to present ourselves. And it is also due to this that we have such appreciation for you.

Humanity is currently at a changing point in history, a time when decisions that have always been made in a certain direction have more probability of being made in a new way. We choose to communicate now because of the aid that we can offer in making these new decisions, which we see as beneficial in regards to what you are claiming to be wanting in your **populus**.

As you continually pray, or ask for, the salvation of your civilization and peoples, we are of the mind that you would like to have the tools to understand how that salvation is going to come about.

The information we share with you is nothing more than stopping someone who is frantically looking for their glasses and telling them: 'They are already on your face'. The tools you seek are and always have been within you. Our communications' main goals are to point you to this knowing in the hopes that you laugh and say 'Oh silly me.' as opposed to insisting that the glasses are not on your nose and pretending, even longer that you do not see.

The glasses are the knowing of your personal power to choose and your face is the state of unity and oneness upon which that rests. At the moment, although you are beginning to look in the mirror, you have not yet realized either of these truths. We hope to catch your attention long enough for you to stop searching and realize that what you were looking for was always there.

We are a present version of All in the space in which we reside. In that space there is no separation, and so we do not see and we do not perceive of separation between us and you in the same way that you perceive of separation between yourselves and us.

Whether it is past or future or present it is all the same. We can say as easily we are a past version of you as we can say we are a past, or present, or future version of you and by you, meaning both you as you are in the situation, and our vessel - All of you, the grand You. Consciousness is all One.

The first and primary theme we present is to:
Help in the understanding of Oneness as oneness includes all.
Our secondary themes would be:
Love and self-love
The advancement of your civilization - relationally, technologically and emotionally
Revealing parts of a more horizontal reality to you that has not been seen yet
The healing through the dissolution of the capacity to hold judgment of ALL of your kind
Each portion of consciousness, or individuation, has its unique signature and in communication, there are unique receptors and transmitters.

WHY DO SOURCES OF WISDOM CONTRADICT?

In order to expand at a more accelerated rate through your species or populus or peoples, there is a requirement for many voices to match the many ears.

There are millions of ears who cannot hear the word 'angel', there are millions of ears who cannot hear the word 'alien', there are millions of ears who cannot hear from the voice of what they perceived of as 'woman', there are millions of ears who cannot hear the voice of what they perceived of as 'man', there are blocks and dams for most ears that will keep them from hearing the One Voice, unless it is peppered and flavored according to their tastes and palate.

A drop of water has a ripple effect and it goes in all directions, and on the pond's surface, it may come across a bug in one direction and change its pattern, in one direction it may come across a leaf or stone and these will affect the ripples but the ripples will continue to reach the shore. The drop of water remains the same regardless of the form of the wave created by its impact with what it has touched.

The message has always been and will always be the same.

Your ancient texts, wisdom writings, prophets, sages and shamans are all simply cooking their own flavor of the same stew.

Now you are stepping into the kitchen and working with the same information. You are rising up towards the source of the one message to bring it down to Earth to flavor your stew in a certain way so that those who want to eat what you have to offer, will have a delicious meal.

We come to you in this way, so that those who want to eat what we have to offer will have a delicious meal.

Your favorite teachers do the same, and do not believe that teaching or channeling are any different from one another, as even the concept of teaching, or the concept of channeling are different flavors of the same stew.

Even one who cradles a baby alone in a dark room at night, is in their own way, cooking their own stew, for the message is the same.

There are some of you who choose to, shall we say, cook for an entire soup kitchen, and others who, keep things very close to home, but the flavor is always yours.

It is beautiful to also see this when looking at **other-selves**, for there is no difference, except for the spices that they've used.

If you can see past the particular spices or the choices or the situations or the potential that the individual has, you can see that it is always consistently Source.

It is so important for us, that you learn to see each other in the way we see you.

We are certain that nothing else needs to be done.

Why Do You Choose to Speak With Us?

There is always some form of agenda. Our agenda is close to the intention of creation - Expansion.

Our choice to speak with you in this way and to create this book with you is in part because of your request to receive this message and to read it. It is necessary in creation for all requests to be fulfilled.

In another part it is our pleasure to speak with you in this way for we see you as us and to interact with another portion of us is entirely satisfying.

If some of the information that you have called through us helps to accelerate your journey and place you in a position of feeling more well more of the time, then this too is our pleasure.

You must remember that every experience that you are having with every other-self is exactly because they have nothing better to do. Every being is experiencing the absolute best experience for them in any moment even if they are not appreciating that.

So if you are talking to a teller at the post office and they are very grumpy with you and it seems as if they want to be somewhere else, they are still exactly where they are meant to be. You may prefer to have a more gregarious teller but you are also where you need to be. You have nowhere better to be.

We also hold a great level of curiosity for your mystery. We envy the possibility to not know as much as we do. From this not-knowing can stem **true creation** as you assemble all the components and weave the threads together in a way that is most pleasing to you. In our existence this is no longer possible as we see all the configurations simultaneously, and so are not surprised by our own novelty, as we choose.

The arts, the way you weave words, and the stories you wrap around relationships and interaction are far more creative than we are capable of.

To you, they are new. This is why so many come to be with you. Although we see each of you as us and all of your infinite possibilities, you yourselves choose in each moment which of those possibilities to apply. For us these choices offer a moment of surprise in an existence that has made surprise unfamiliar. We thank you, as you are the best show on TV, so to speak. For we do not know the ending of this show. We do not know what you'll do next. It is all up to you.

Consider a simple house cat. As all things, it is part of the universal consciousness. It is as likely that the cat holds the wisdom of all of the cosmos or universes, or eternity as it would be that some channeled energy would hold that wisdom. Perhaps in reflecting on this, one can bring themselves back to a certain balance, where there is understanding that there is no difference between something that one has decided is insignificant or beneath them and what one has decided is more significant or above them. By this reflection, one can see that inside all things lies the same wisdom.

The nice trick that you could extract from this understanding would be to find that thing for which you feel the most reverence. Find that thing to which you give the most authority. Then breathe into the feelings that come with that reverence and sense of authority and understand that these feelings and these sensations could not exist without you.

In this way, you are automatically removing the focus from the object of your affection and placing it back onto the source in which it comes. Once that is completed, all of the attributes that you have attached to that wisdom, or authority, reveal themselves to be within you. You are not able to have an experience that is not generated from within. This includes any mystical experiences, it includes relational experiences. It is inclusive of all that you see, feel, taste, smell, hear, touch and sense.

WHAT DENSITY ARE YOU FROM?

We are from a non-space-time that holds oneness in that complete reverence. We love in a way that is beyond the physical capabilities of matter. We do not exist in space-time but time-space, and we are completely aware of our limitlessness. These characteristics are shared by many, and touched upon by some in many densities.

The numerical names and explanations associated with 'density' that have been made available to you are imperfect as they are based in language, which is symbol, and not truth. In this same way you never actually see a river when you look at what you have labeled as 'river'. 'River' is a representation in language of the movement of water, so there is no actual river until you say there is, and even then there is no river but the idea or concept of one.

You are not seeing the reality beyond your labels which are all fictitious. The same understanding could be applied to the conceptual descriptions which have been placed upon What-Is, for convenience sake.

How Many Beings Are in Your Entity Group?

There are no many in the One. And yet, communication again here restricts our freedom to express the truth as truth. From where we are looking, we know that the **simultaneous realities** of our existence and this moment are possible only because of an observation of it. So the 'We' when we refer to ourselves in this way, is you.

However, if one believes themselves to be an individual, they project individuality onto what they see. We make concessions for this difference in understanding.

What Planet Are You From?

We do not see your planetary existence in the way that you do. We see the beings on what you are calling a planet as a part of us. We do not see a separation between you and us at all. Nor do we see a separation between your animals, and bacteria, trees, rocks, plastics, waters, gases, atoms.

All of those things that you've given names to, and separated from you, we do not see as separate from us. It is hard to describe what one sees or feels about a part of oneself, without performing the act of separation from oneself. We know we tread in the grounds of paradox as if we are not separate, then how and why are we speaking to ourselves?

But this is the beautiful spiral of the illusion. For a part of you knows that you are not what you think you are. That part of you did not arrive at awareness knowing or thinking that it was on a planet or that it was human or that it was male or female or that it had limits or boundaries.

You go to the moment of your birth all that you know is that you **are**.

This is how we see you. We see you from that optic of 'I Am'. This is the energy of what you know closest as 'love'. When one sees from the eyes of 'I Am' anything that one can rest their eyes upon, rest their ears upon, rest their hand upon, smell or feel or taste is them. And so to come to the 'why' we communicate with you; although completely unnecessary in one part it is also the most loving action possible on the other. And those two parts are the whole.

We will let you know that the understanding of planets is a material understanding and therefore any being from what you would call a **density** level that does not identify with their material form would say that you were from another planet, not inferring that they themselves had a planet, but that you believed that you did. This is why the term 'extra-terrestrial' is not so much applicable to beings from other planets as it is simply to those that do not identify with yours.

We have understood your concepts of planets and do not feel the necessity to either confirm or deny our connection with one or any mass of rock anywhere in any of the galaxies for our primary identification with location is non-location. Our consciousness is at a state where it is not limited by location or physical form in this present Now and, as now is all there is, there is no need to confuse or distract our conversation with discussion of provenance. These concepts tie into a linearity that is coming undone in its understanding, as it is not of optimal functioning.

We do not reside in the ways that you would imagine. We do not exist in a framework that allows for location in the ways that you would imagine and so the answer becomes quite complicated and yet extremely simple.

We are nowhere and everywhere. We are you. We are us. We are it. We are then. We are now. We are All and though you have consistent use of human physical vessels, so are you.

We know that there is such a desire to locate and understand to perhaps use your fabulous minds to draw conclusions and explanations and we admire so much your courage in this journey of no answers.

Do You Have a Physical Form?

Likewise, to be able to be seen in physical form, one would need to position oneself in space and time in order to have contrast between the energy field and what is not the energy field. There is the capability of many non-physical beings to materialize physically or, to present themselves in a physical form, to whomever would choose to see them in that form. It does not answer the question as to whether or not we are primarily non-physical or whether or not we are what you would call 'alien' it simply answers the question of our capability of visual representation. It is not our preference or currently in favor of our contract with you to position ourselves in space-time if not only in certain circumstances. Please note that to be able to be seen we do require the consent of the free will of the one who is seeing. Which ultimately, is always you.

Have You Ever Been Incarnate on Earth in a Past Life?

As we have access to more of the universal consciousness than you do from your perspective we can say 'Yes', however we do not identify with this experience directly or these multitudes of experiences directly as they are both a part of what we are and individuation is to which we have access.

We have what you would call incarnations, that are closer to us, in what could be seen as a personal nature. However, as we do not associate with personal nature at this time. It is more of a flavor, a knowing, an under-standing, of what that was/is. As each experience is an experience in the oneness of **All-That-Is** and we exist in a space beyond time you could say that all incarnations, past, present and future are directly our experience and the wisdom that we draw from.

You could say that your author/the vessel is also one of these incarnations and so by your definitions, you may consider us a future version or higher version of the vessel, this is why we are able to connect relatively seamlessly. You may also say that they or even you are a future version of us and it is you in this moment recalling wisdom from what you would call a **past life**.

So we can describe to you, if need be, one or many of these parallel existences that you would consider in your past or future to be earth incarnations and from our perspective we would not see them linearly and would not see them as personal and yet nothing could be more personal as All is included in the One.

We are fortunate to be able to tap into all these experiences in order to have a broader perspective as we have access to the experience of the many in the One. Each of these experiences inclusive of your experience adds to the expansion of the One. You are fortunate in this way as well and can too tap into this wisdom with practice, intention, surrender and will.

We have so much love for you. We have so much desire to be able to express that in a way that you can understand but we have limitations in this way we have answered more than the question.

I share Vagrein's message with you now in the hopes that your journey too comes from a place of seeking to rest in that place of sharing. We all have very unique gifts to offer humanity and each one of us, encouraged to be our whole beautiful selves, is a fundamental contributing factor to creating the world we want to live in tomorrow.

We would like to begin by talking with you about the journey of 'remembering who you are'. This is an inaccurate definition for what your actual human journey is. The true You never forgot who you are and so there is nothing for it to remember. What happened can more concretely be described as a 'who you are not', was constructed upon and over the who you are.

We can label, for convenience sake, 'who you are not' as the **ego** or the person. This 'ego' is synonymous with 'separation' and can be described as any form of separation in its myriad of forms.

It is any and every moment in which you believe yourself to separate from the whole. It is any and every thought in which you believe yourself to separate from the whole. It is any and every action in which you believe yourself to separate from the whole.

Humans, feeling they are bound by their physical form, are taught that they are separate because of their physical form. The ideas that the physical form is delicate and that death in a finite nature, is possible, introduces fear into the mind of man. From this place of fear it is easy to believe that one is separate as fear would merit defense and protection from the non-preferable outcome of death.

The confusion introduced with the ideas and the belief systems allow one to make colossal sacrifices of the majority of what they truly are, what life is and what they have come here to experience.

There is no escape from ego, your identity as a person or separation itself, from within the game of the ego. There's also no need to escape from within that perspective for only separation could believe in the need to escape. When one returns to the whole, there is no ego and there is nothing to fight. Not even one's ideas of themselves.

We are proposing to you the choice of forgetting separation. The only death you will experience, if you choose to forget, is the death of all the perceived limitations you have been facing in your life. They cannot exist without the belief in separation. The ego will die, but as it does, life as it truly is will be avail-

Forgetting Who You Are Not

able for you to perceive for the first time. You will be able to see yourself as you truly are for the first time.

This 'who you are not' is a constructed being and not you at all. It never has been. This being was never the true you to begin with and therefore holds no memories of your true essence. Separation does not have the ability to remember who you are. It will never find who you truly are. It will not remember. The seeking is set up to be perpetual.

Luckily, the who you **are** was never actually lost. The construct does not need to remember. It only needs to forget and be forgotten. To access and uncover what was never lost, all you need to do is to forget everything you have learnt since you have been here. Everything you remember points to and reinforces the ego or separation.

They were all lies, and yet, also allies. The challenges you set up for yourself as a child and the misunderstandings with your other-selves in the form of your parents and peers were necessary at the time to motivate you to the point you find yourself in now. In this way, everything, perceived either as good or as bad, that has led to this exact moment was serving you at the highest level. At this moment, however, they are no longer needed.

Forget what 'the experts' tell you. Trust yourself. Those you call experts are amplifiers of what has come before now and often what has come before now has not worked or been holistic or functional. They have risen to their positions by most faithfully regurgitating what has been told, in turn to them. Stop the chain of misinformation.

There is no person on this planet who can know anything better than you can. You are your only expert. Have faith in this and faith in yourself and you will never need an expert again.

Remember that the books from which the experts have learnt are written by the same **consciousness** that you have access to Now. The experiments and tests and focus groups that they draw their statistics from are created by humans. The books were written by humans. The experiments conducted by humans.

We do not want to diminish humans here, and introduce the idea that had they been written by some other beings, they would have more authority. We are not. We are simply stating that you are the only authority on YOU.

Are not the textbooks changing faster and faster now? Is this not an indication that everything you have learnt about your world, your classifications and naming systems and conventions, are not the fixed truth that they are proposed to be? Are they all not proven inaccurate shortly after going to print? Your scientific frontier is all about separating and explaining the 'why everything is' and then drawing conclusions on how to manipulate that why for your means. The true answer to the question 'Why is this?' is always the same.

It is.

You study the past as if it is going to help you to understand and choose the preferred future but have no evidence of this ever having been the case. You repeat the past by repeating the past. You choose the future by creating new intentions towards it.

Do not be fooled. Question each new piece of information offered to you as if it was food. Decide whether or not you want to put that information into your body, spending the energy and time processing and digesting it. Begin the detoxification of your being by forgetting everything you think you know.

The only thing you truly 'know' is existence. All the knowledge that belongs to you was born with you. Straying from what you know to be true for you will only lead to confusion, doubt, slowing of your growth, separation and eventually disease.

The difference between a teaching and a doctrine is that the one who is teaching is not invested in whether or not you adopt what they are offering as true. You may choose to learn from teachings. Seek out the knowledge or wisdom of those who came before you to save time and learn any practical tools that you would, but never make them your own. Learning to discern what information feeds separation and what feeds unity or love, will also aid in you understanding what it is you would like to adopt.

You may forget all the social rules and the patterns of behavior around interacting. Most of them are not conducive to unity or real relating-ship with other-selves. Rituals and habits in interaction with other-selves only bring with them in-authenticity towards true connection. You may see everything as a written script. And the conversations around you as being automated. Question them, question yourself. You will find that separation keeps you more automated than not.

Question your own reactions to things. Favor response to reaction in all cases. Look, listen and feel. Question your feelings. They are always telling you how far or close you are to forgetting. When you have forgotten separation and you are not in the talons of ego, you will be feeling good. When you are in any form of separation, you will be feeling bad.

Your feelings are not important in the way that you believe them to be. They are fundamental, but the importance has been confused. We will dedicate a chapter further in this volume to the thinking, feeling mind and untangle their functionality, proposing a new interaction with them that allows you to remain in unity and love.

Forget all the labels you have been given or give to yourself. You are fresh and new in each moment and are nothing that you believe yourselves to be. You are nothing. No-thing.

You are not a man or a woman, a student, a profession, you are not a colour of skin or an age or a size, you are not your body or your mind or your accomplishments. You are not a nationality. These labels do not actually even exist. They are man-made. If you were alone on the planet would you need to categorize so distinctly? If you were alone now would separation serve you?

What is a nation but a squiggly line drawn on a visual representation of your topography? If you were the only One, would nations exist? What is a skin colour but a different genetic disposition for handling melanin in the metabolic process. If you were the only One, would skin just be skin? What is sex but a different configuration of genitalia for the purpose of procreation. If you were the only One, would the entirety of the not body be revered for the amazing tool and vehicle that it is with gratitude and appreciation in any configuration?

You are not the experiences you have had. You are not a victim. You are not guilty. You are nothing.

The moment you label yourself you limit yourself. How can you make any categorical statements about yourself when there is no one thing that can express the All-ness of your being? Forget the labels that cause separation. They do not serve. You may forget the labels that others choose to put onto you to define you. You are energy and vibration alone, and even those two labels fail to represent the entirety of your being.

Do not fear the freedom you have always had to not define yourself. Do not fear the freedom that comes when these definitions drop. Do not fear the love that flows into the entirety of your being when the labels and descriptions you have of other-selves and the world around you dissolve into the All-That-Is.

As you forget everything you think you are, you gain access to your unique gift to existence.

Forgetting is the shortcut towards your own choosing of understanding of the meaning of life. If you forget what you are not, you finally have access to the knowledge of why you decided to come to incarnation in this specific time-space illusion.

You have not forgotten what your gift, purpose or mission is, you just do not see the value of it yet. You may believe that your gift is somehow less important or not useful, or not exciting, or that you will never have access to it. You do not have access to it because of the beliefs of this shadowy constructed figure of separation that has been lain upon it. You all know what your gifts are and can live as them when the not-you is forgotten and stops covering them.

As they are revealed, they are as obvious to you as your hands. They are not lost or unknown, forgotten or hidden. Your gift is Who You Are. Who You Are is your gift. As soon as you stop judging, or trying to fix, or change, your actions will reflect who you are, and your gift will flow through you. There is not one gift. The being IS the gift. Your work, if there was work, would be to get out of the way forgetting everything that is not the gift.

As you make this choice, the separation shifts, it moves. Your natural activations begin. The holy and purified version that you so want to be is no longer out of arm's reach. It seems to come to you effortlessly. We say 'seems', because it is an illusion that it comes to you as it had never left, and was never anywhere other than where you are, it being you.

To provide such a high reward, one would think that this forgetting would be complicated however you are already a master at forgetting. Forgetting is one of the easiest things possible.

You forget everything at night when you go to sleep. When you are full of joy and you are doing what you love; you forget. When you are concentrating on something that interests you; you forget. When you are with people that you care about; you forget.

You remember to identify with the construct when you have nothing else going on. The complacency reminds you of every perceived bad choice 'you' ever made, all those who called you unworthy, the problems and nagging thoughts in your mind. When you are not aligned, you remember to be guilty or shameful or unworthy or any of your favorite emotions because you remember in that moment that you are supposed to think you are

Someone.

But who told you that you are supposed to think you are someone? They did not know, and it was a lie.

Your parents taught you your name, but it was not yours. They taught you your gender but there was no proof of this since gender is a concept. They taught you your nationality, whether you were good or bad, what your religion was. They told you what it meant to be smart and what it meant to be stupid. They told you what it meant to be special and unimportant. They taught you "this is what it means to be a person and this is what it means to be alive", but you already knew something different about that, didn't you?

As a small child, before all of those lessons, you knew what it felt like to be alive, and no one had to tell you.

So forget what they told you, because before they did, you already knew. Your negative feelings can only come back in when you are not in touch with that truth, because that baby knew nothing of guilt or shame, fear, unworthiness, separation. How could it?

A moment will arrive when you simply forget everything other than who you are. This will be a moment of clarity and grace.

It will feel, perhaps, like a remembering, but really it is what could be lifted being removed from you and given back to its rightful owner as the illusion it always was. All your thoughts about yourself, all your perceptions, everything that keeps you small and away from yourself, never belonged to you. It all belongs to the What-Is, as do you as the true Who You Are.

There will be a knowing inside of each of you where there is pure existence, and that same existence never left. It just got piled under the clutter. Now, if you go look for it. You will find it there. It has not moved. At the bottom of the pile of stinky laundry is You.

This will be when you choose, but you must choose for this moment to arrive for it to come.

We will talk many times in this volume about how you are choosing your own reality. We will talk about fate and destiny, free will and predetermined outcomes. We will show how these are not polar concepts. That will is fate and will is faith. Choice creates your destiny and the only true choice is surrendering to destiny.

The forgetting of what you are not, or the remembering of what you are, requires only you choosing to do so. Once that choice is made, the doing, or rather,the unfolding of the circumstances to arrive at your chosen desire, are not of your doing.

It needs not be done. It already Is.

You may not think you have the power to make this choice. You may not know why you chose to come to this experience. At times you may even regret having made that choice because in your confusion, you do not see the purity, purpose and beauty of it.

Tap into that moment - that one beautiful moment, when you touched that first cell, and said "Divide." Tap into that one glorious moment before your heart first beat and you said "Beat" When you feel the love, energy and power you had in those moments when you made those choices, your doubts, fears and ideas of separation are immediately erased and forgotten. The choice is remade in this moment as it was in that.

Fears become laughable and your pain turns into what it truly has been trying to show to you: the immense love that you came here with.

You are beautiful and powerful and we are in awe.

**B**eyond and before all distractions, is silence.

The 'All-That-Is' is exactly what it sounds to be - All-That-Is. We describe this now for you in this chapter in order to better be able to understand the rest of this document.

All-That-Is is What-Is.

It is all that one can and does experience, all that one can and does know, all that one can and does feel, all that one can and does sense, all that one can and does think. It includes all - All within and without perception.

It is every blade of grass. It is every grain of sand. It is every drop in the ocean and includes everyone one of you.

All-That-Is is the all inclusivity that the exclusivity of separation attempts to divide.

All-That-Is includes the idea of separation. It includes the concept of ego.

You are not only a part of the All-That-Is but simultaneously All-That-Is. You cannot be apart from the All-That-Is.

You are all that you see. You are all that you touch. You are all that you hear. You are all you sense, all you smell, all you taste and all that is beyond your senses. All that you see, all that you touch, all you sense, all you hear, all you smell, all you taste and all that is beyond your senses is all the What-Is. There is no exclusion, nothing left out and nothing that is beyond its encompassing.

You may ask 'What is it that is able to perceive All-That-Is?' and we will say that that too is an element of All-That-Is and cannot be separated from any aspect of the All-That-Is for that would make it something other than what is which cannot be. All-That-Is is all that is and also all that can be.

We asked you to make an effort to understand that this truly is all inclusive for the reason that it nullifies the very common sense of unworthiness amongst your people. It nullifies the sense of separation amongst your people.

All-That-Is is the only truth. It is synonymous with unity. It is synonymous with Oneness. It is

THE ALL-THAT-IS IS ALL-THAT-IS

synonymous with God in many of the ways that you choose to understand that word and also in the many ways you do not. And it is synonymous with sound and silence. All comes back to the All-That-Is.

We will talk about several subjects as this text continues. At times it may seem as if these subjects are separate from one another. It may seem that they are different from one another. We assure you that they are not and that it is only because you are a part of All-That-Is and because you are All-That-Is that you have any access to be able to even contemplate these subjects and imagine them to be separate from each other.

Whether they are health, or relationships, or science, or the cosmology and past, future and present of your people's history, or even what We are, all, in all ways come back to What-Is.

As you read this book, as you continue, if you can hold this thought in your mind even if you do not yet understand it completely, you will be able to absorb the information without the seeming blockage of separation that you hold within your confusion.

This time is blessed, for so many for so many voices of the One Voice are spinning off in fractals and they're able to reach into spaces that they could not reach earlier. When listening carefully enough, it is clear it is One Voice and the message is less important than the understanding of the One Voice. Then beyond the One Voice is the one silence.

It is in that silence that the solution for all of your perceived problems finds its resolution. For in that silence, there is no air for your problems to breathe. There is no land for your problems to stand on. There is only the end-of-standing of the silence.

Complete faith in existence and Self arrive through the recognition of What-Isness - the isness of everything that is. As recognition helps in the disassembling of various levels of importance of the elements within the What-Is.

There are no one or several or many things in the What-Is that have more importance than others for they are all One and equal in importance. Each element has infinite significance and insignificance simultaneously.

Each experience affects the collective consciousness and so any and every experience affects it. To imagine that an experience affects it any differently than any other experience is giving importance or significance to something over something else when all is equal in terms of energetics and influence on the collective. All is needed for the collective.

We would like to underline that there are no personal questions or subjects. For at its core it is impossible for anything to be personal. Consciousness is One and by adopting anything that flows through consciousness as your own or personal or separate from the rest of the All makes things difficult for you. If you were to re-frame your experiences and queries as part of the whole and All-That-Is choosing to have that experience, you will have relief, faster.

By the time that you finish the reading of this book, we **augur** that you hold even a fraction deeper the knowing of inter-connectivity. Knowing the infinite reach of the All-That-Is is the key to knowing oneself and to understanding the perfection that **scintillates** throughout existence.

We now outline what service is, why you have that desire, what's the purpose of your individuated existence and how to bring your own unique expression into clearer focus for yourself and other-selves. Desire, in general, does not come from you. You do not choose your desires.

It is the Creator, or All-That-Is which chooses your desires. They come upon you unannounced. They are not researched and purchased. One day you awake, and they are there, existing alongside every other experience and perception. A higher wisdom knows which desires and fires to light within you. If a desire exists in you, it is your path.

Perhaps knowing this will aid in the unblocking any blockage you believe yourself to have in regards to being in service.

We are excited that there is interest in spicing your stew.

You may release what you believe to be blocking you from being in service at any time you choose to may and begin to be who you came here to be.

If you believe that your voice does not contribute in the way that you would like, despite the decision of the All-That-Is (*that it ∙oes*), it may be because you, through your studies, or accumulation of knowledge external to your knowing, have chosen to create, or distill, concepts and thought constructs which allow you to address this belief head-on.

Are you ready to be what you came here to be? Are you ready to choose to be what you came here to be? And are you presently choosing a reality in which you will have the illusion of no longer having the luxury to choose?

We see you edging towards that choice and we see how you have all got your spandex uniforms and capes ready to become the superheroes that you are. It will mean giving up the idea that you're anything but what you came here to be.

Those who read this message did not come to enjoy themselves, even if there is joy to be had. Your joy is the service. As is ours

Deep within each of your hearts you know who you are. You know what you came here to be. You have an idea of who you are, not as an identity, not as a per-

BEING WHO YOU CAME HERE TO BE

son, not as your name, your actions, your behaviors, the things you do in your day-to-day life but who you are. The miracle that you are, the essence and the power and the intention of your life. You have an idea deep within you of who you are.

For many of you this is terrifying because you believe that if you allow yourself the luxury of knowing it or choosing it you would not be able to live up to that idea.

It's absurd. You have allowed yourself to be convinced that you are not who you already know yourself to be. You have strength and power and the ability to lead, you have the ability to heal, you have the ability to aid, what needs to be aided without looking for people to save.

You have the ability to absorb all of the concepts and all of the teachings that you have already heard and taught to yourself on a visceral level. You have all been studying for a long time and all know that whatever has resonated with you has come from you. Everything that you admire in the external world, everything that you've seen that you have found to be beautiful, all of these things with which you have resonated in your entire life are simply signals of the beauty and the magnificence and the possibility and capability of you as yourself. Whatever you see outside of yourself that feels good is You, that You that you came here to be.

A leaf is no more special than a branch. A branch no more special than the roots. There can be no part of a whole that is special.

The words that are used to describe can fool you into thinking that something could be better than something else. Who made the rules of one thing being better than another thing? Who decided?

When you see something that stands out, such as a being that stands out, it is similar to seeing the part of a plant that stands out. While seeing the flower with its vibrant colour, its fragrant smell you focus your attention on the flower and say it is special. You say it is desirable because you are like a bee. You're busy. Busy buzzing and looking for benefits. It is because you are trying to get something that you are attracted to the flower and its vibrant colour and fragrant smell. They exist to attract you. The flower could not be without the rest of the plant. It could not be without the water that feeds its roots, coming in the form of rain. The flower could not be without the sunshine or the minerals of the earth. It could not even be without you, you busy bee. A flower could not be without the bee who wants something from it. All of it is special. Yet it is overlooked because one is distracted by the illusion of importance.

You are looking in one direction and giving it importance simply because you have decided for it to be. You feel like there is benefit. You feel like there is pollen. So you try to get to the flower. All the time forgetting that the flower is only a flower because it needs you. It only exists in its splendor and in its glory because of you. The whole plant needs you. It's all connected. Down in the root system - all the worms and the dead organic matter swirl together in a perfected and intricate dance. This is a metaphor of everything, every moment, ever scenario, every situation, everything you see can only be because you see it. The will of the bee. You have such a desire to serve you overlook how you are already serving. You want more because somehow you were convinced that more is better. More is the flower. You don't need more avenues to serve. Your service exactly as you are is enough. You are enough.

There's nothing to do once you make this choice. It will all be done for you, but it does involve letting go of everything that you are not.

It involves letting go of the opinions that others have of you. It involves letting go of anyone who would not approve. It involves letting go of those things that you already know do not serve you - it might be a job, it might be a relationship, it might be a location. You know these things.

There's no one who is going to tell you who you are. You know who you are. You are just pretending not to. Instead of allowing yourselves to be fully who you are, you are choosing circumstances which push you into a situation where you no longer have to choose because you will have to be who you are or else. This is not a warning. It is just what is happening and it is demonstrated by your newsreels. The idea of violence that is increasing around you is not happening outside of you. It is what you are choosing.

You are choosing it so that you can become who you are.

You want to have the opportunity to rise to the occasion because without the occasion you do not believe you could rise.

We are saying that you can.

You can rise to the occasion without the occasion.

We do not judge. There is no better or worse, though you would see it that way. Either way is perfect.

If you would like to imagine a crisis, who are you in that crisis situation? Are you cowering in a corner? Or are you helping people out of the burning building? Are you wondering what they think of you? Or are you busy organizing transport to get away from the militants? We know you to be heroes. All of you. We know you to be the best versions of humanity when you choose to be, when you feel like you have no choice and the goodness that is within spills out to compensate for the darkness you see. This is what we are meaning by choosing and at the time to choose is now. And now. And now.

It's time to let go of anything that is not your highest version with such love and appreciation and gratitude for how it has kept you all these years.

What if, up until this moment your life has been the tutorial version of the program of being You and now the controls have been handed over to you by the programmer who said:

"Well now you know what to do, do what you like."

Or more accurately:

"The tutorial level of this game is complete, would you like to begin the real game?"

Of course you can play the tutorial as many times as you like. Until you feel comfortable that you know where all the functions are or you could just dive into the game and see what happens, hope that you remember where the different functions are hiding in the interface.

Humanity does not need to be saved and there is no one to serve.

There is no one truly to save. There is a game that you have chosen to come here to play in which you are the heroes. You can at any moment circumvent the whole thing but then you would not have the opportunity to be what you came here to be and that comes back to this concept of being a hero.

If you chose tomorrow to end all of the suffering of the planet you could. All you would have to do is nothing except 'Be' it into awareness.

There are some amazing things happening and you get to be a part of that. That is why you came and it is so exciting and the time is now.

And yet, you have this desire to serve. Perhaps you don't know what your mission is. Perhaps you don't hear your calling.

You came here with the desire to be of service. You cannot know why you have been created the way that you were created, you were just created that way, there is some service waiting to be had within you.

You can feel it deep within yourself and yet, if All-is-One, which it is, how could there possibly be anyone to serve? If all is perfection, which it is, how could any one of your actions or any elements of your being here affect that perfection in any way at all?

Why did you come with a sensation that life should have meaning? Why is there a burning fire inside of you that tells you to search for that meaning and where is it found?

When you have a belief about what your service will be in this world it is keeping you within a box that does not actually correlate with your true service. Your service is your moment to moment experience of being in touch with your heart.

There are no words that will soothe what you have chosen to carry as yours. This is the same for any belief or concept on any topic throughout your lives. No experience or word will save you from the burden of your own decisions. Nothing that can be taken from outside to relieve an internal burning, but perhaps one can be gentle and slowly come to soothe oneself. You may of course, use experience, teachings and messages such as these to cross-reference what you are doing internally but never imagine that it was the experience or words that changed something for you. It was only ever your choice to change.

It is a delicate business, for you to refuse to tolerate the addition of doubt on a mental plane, in what you know to be true in your heart. You seem to have a world of evidence to the less than optimum conditions. This 'evidence' adds to already deeply conditioned negative thought patterns and you are in a dance, daily, attempting to side step these thoughts, for you know that there are more productive and more beautiful thoughts to occupy your mind with. There is a discord between these seeming negative thoughts and what you already know to be true. Your role here is to align your thoughts with the truth so that you may embody the truth and share the light of the truth with more of yourself as the whole.

So, our friendly advice would be to decide differently.

In the case of the vessel and narrator, it has been useful to experiment with what she would call powers such as energy healing, mind reading, astral projection and telepathy, in order to build confidence to arrive at where she, and all of you, already are.

This is unnecessary and yet common, and perfectly orchestrated by this non-separated portion of the All-That-Is.

One needs only decide what they want. However there is a tendency to claim one does not know what they want.

If you doubt whether your service has meaning, it has no meaning. If you do not doubt its meaning, magically it has meaning. The relevance for you would be the one you would choose for it to have. You can decide to not doubt the relevance.

If you were, tomorrow, to believe that your actions could cure cancer and believe it deep enough, there would be no tumors left and that would be your relevance.

It is your belief system and your choosing of your belief system that controls the reality you can perceive. Therefore changing your beliefs would automatically transform what you see into your preference. Instead of wondering what you have come here to do in order to be in service you would simply choose to be doing it already and for it to be of the utmost importance.

It is helpful to be able to be aware of your belief system and decide if it is serving you or not. There are no negative beliefs per sè, but there are beliefs that are serving or not serving.

It is important not to get too attached to beliefs. You can be spontaneous and flexible with the decisions that you make in your life. If you can easily let go of those that do not serve by detaching your sense of self, which is the false self you continue to remember to paste upon your being as you awake each day, then it becomes simple to see something is not serving and to replace it with something that does.

Pay attention to the thought forms and emotions that are coming up around you sharing your work. Be diligent in sorting out which thoughts are serving you and which are not and do not tolerate any thought forms that do not lead you in the direction of your desire.

As you desire is to be in service in the brightest way for the most beings possible, know that any thought forms relating to how you, in your person-identity, are perceived, are in contrast to this goal.

It would be well to focus, while conscious, on the feeling state of your goal, for some time, in a daily meditation to strengthen your immunity to thought forms that distract you from this deep desire. We will discuss what thought forms are later in this text and give you some keys to understand and untangle yourselves from them.

Thoughts create beliefs. Thoughts are part of the All-That-Is and therefore cannot be yours exclusively.

You are not a victim to any thought, belief, emotion or circumstance. You are never a victim.

This choice of phrase can be triggering because when one feels wronged by emotion or belief or circumstances, there is the natural desire for compassion.

We hold that compassion for you more than you choose to hold it for yourself. If you were truly compassionate with yourself, you would see that continuing to remain in the mentality of victim-hood, as if something apart from you or something apart from the All-That-Is could influence you negatively, is actually harming you more than circumstances ever did or could.

Feeling the triggering in this, as in every, case is actually in itself the ultimate benevolence as well, for it will ultimately lead you to understand that you are not a victim.

At any time one is believing themselves to be anything other than the whole of creation, special, weird, different, apart, superior, inferior, they are automatically in a state that is not serving themselves or the whole.

If you have a desire to live a life in service to humanity, which many, many of you reading this do, you are past the point where you can believe in separation without that being painful for you.

When you have seeming negative or painful feelings you can be certain that it is because you have stretched your understanding of reality further than it had previously been and that your thoughts or actions are not yet in alignment with the new understanding. Have some gentle compassion for yourself in this phase as you are undoing lifetimes of habits.

To believe yourself to be a victim will become more and more painful as you step further into your full being as you are understanding more and more how separation cannot be possible.

This is what you asked for and what you have worked for in this incarnation. It does mean however that any wavering from this understanding at all will bring course correction in the form of feelings and experiences on a much swifter rate.

When it comes to your life's path, or blueprint, calling, mission, et cetera there is no need to preoccupy yourself with 'How to do anything'. It is done. The 'how' you will experience that is of your choosing and will come naturally.

All connects and flows in perfect timing, including your collaboration with other-selves and the moment that you select your intention to follow through with that desire, you will be able to do so without any obstacles.

The frequency of excitement is definitely beneficial to acceleration in any factor. There is nothing specific that you need to do to make yourself faster than you are. This is all happening very naturally and at the pace in which it is perfect for you. There is no need to arrive where you believe that you are going faster than you are arriving there.

Understand that where you are is perfect in the moment and apply that same excitement to the moment that you are currently living, as opposed to projecting it onto a future that you believe is somehow better than this present.

You do not have any part in the speed of which your messages or service are received, as they will be received in exactly the precise moment to each precise portion of consciousness for which they are meant. It is all calculated to be delivered in accordance with the optimal outcome, of the highest timeline for all.

Every portion of consciousness is in service to all other portions of consciousness. You are each other being simultaneously. You are us simultaneously as we are you. You are all of your previous versions and all of your future versions and all of your potential versions as well as everyone else's. The vastness of this concept is infinite and we would suggest meditation upon it.

So you may feel special, or important, or proud if you choose to be in service for other-selves, however you can only feel these things if you do not understand that it is simply you who is helping yourself. Once you understand that, you open a doorway to appreciation and gratitude of self and of other-self for all that other-self is doing for you. This understanding facilitates the only true service.

Have complete faith that through this storm all of the desires that you believe you are renouncing will turn, as they always do, into the blooms of the same desires. Always one day too late, perhaps, but we would argue that it is always in perfect timing, for if the results of your efforts arrived the day before your efforting, you would not have put in the effort and the results would not be forthcoming. In other words, while nothing is necessary and cause and effect are often arbitrary, they are never casual.

You are already the most brilliant, sparkling and shining highest form of humanity that you can be.

The work that you are required to do now is that of self acceptance and self realization, so you can see this sparkling beauty in the same way that source sees you. This is the highest service you can provide to humanity, this is the highest service that any being within humanity can provide to humanity for this **unconditional love**, this perfected love for self and other-self is what will unify all of humanity, is what will cease the behaviours that are required to catalyze humanity to make the choice to step into this love.

There are several variations of beings who choose to incarnate on your planet. One variation of those beings does not come to their planet for themselves. These beings holds the desire to be in service of those who are wanting to have the human experience. Their role is not to accumulate experience but to gift what they have accumulated in the past, which is not the past, but simply another version in the time-space illusion continuum.

You cannot **not** be of service. You are already by your simple intention to be of service. In your everyday activities you are already highly in service to others even if you cannot yet see the fruits of the seeds that you are currently planting.

Any sense of confusion and disorientation comes more from your conditioning of what service may or may not look like within your planetary construction and less so from the internal knowing that you have that you are of service. In the lifting of this conditioning you will be able to have more clarity of your innate desire and direction based upon your passions and accumulated skills. You will be more free to serve in the manner that is appropriate and pleasing to you.

There is teaching that suggests that one needs to purify the self before one can be of service however this is not the case for the self is always purified. The self is always the most pure expression of the 'All-That-Is' coming through existence at this time-space. It is only who you are not that can attempt to be purified and only on the level of the 'not-Self'.

Knowing this one may forgive simultaneously self and other-self due to the fact that nothing is ever anything other than the All-That-Is, or the What-Is or the divine choice of what one would call God if one decided to use that word for this concept.

ENERGETIC FORMS OF SERVICE

An energetic act of service may be loving someone even silently, who has never been loved before. It may be sending the vibration of acceptance to one who cannot accept them-self, and it may also involve the energetic forms of healing, of communication, and other non physical abilities that come from one's non physical senses.

If you follow the flow of your own energy and your own experience then you will understand and come into a space where it is more natural for you to have contact with energetic realms as opposed to physical work. You are capable of doing much work on an energetic level if you are able to allow for your discomfort of people thinking that you are doing nothing. If you are in your highest alignment and it does not appear in this world as something tangible then you are , regardless doing your highest work. We are moving with you into a space, a time, or time-line, that will require these energetic anchor points. There is less of a need now for interactive service than there is for the anchor points which will ground and protect and calm the beings who cannot find their own **grounding**, protection and calm.

Your true desires take you naturally to do what you are called to do. A desire to create simply for the sake of creation is most likely based upon a fear that if one does not do, then their worth or permission to be here, is somehow compromised.

You do not need permission to be here. You are already here. You have already gained the permission you need to be exactly as you are. If and when creation is to come through you it will come through you naturally. Up until that point there is absolutely no necessity for you to force or try or effort at all in any way towards creation for the reason you are here is to be exactly as you are

There are those who seem to apply effort in their lives but for them it is not actually an effort because it is just what they are naturally doing. It is easy for those who are naturally taking aligned actions to seem to be impactful. It is easy for them to look at someone who works on an energetic level and misunderstand the entire situation. You all need each other. The one who is doing it needs the one who is still.

Understand this so completely that when you embody it the other-selves with which you spend time will see your true value. Once you see your own true value you can transmit it to other-selves. It is only based upon a level of insecurity as to what you are supposed to be doing that there's even the possibility for anyone to imply or infer that you are not doing what you are 'supposed to be doing'. It is your own insecurity that makes them imply or infer those things for you are the creator of them as well. They are there as an example to show you what you are not so that you can understand what you are.

Yes, this form of service does not have the bells and whistles and glory of some of the other paths that others have chosen but we remind you that you are equally all of the other-selves that you see around you. You are the ultimate creator of the examples that you see around you. You may at any time, if you so choose, take credit for any of the actions that you see any of your other-selves doing as it is you who has created them to be doing those actions in your experience. You are simultaneously someone who can relax completely into the moment and can watch as your friends, lovers, partners and children go off and do, what you can then label as fantastic things in the world, knowing that it is all you.

Silence is an important tool for this work if only just to listen to what you already know. The service provided by one who is an energetic example is as valuable as anyone who may be upon a stage or anyone who builds houses in poor countries. It is valuable because those who are meant to build houses in poor countries will understand, by energetic confidence and example that this is what they are meant to do.

ou are at the maximum growth on the soul level. Any perception or idea, that you are not, is simply a concept introducing an impossibility, into your consciousness. It is impossible to grow more than you are growing for you are the very edge of consciousness. You are the element that has not been seen before. Your existence is expansion itself. How many people before you have been you ?

You cannot be anything other than what you are, no matter what you do and therefore there is nothing that is needed to do.

There is no medal of honour, for striving, working harder, jumping through hoops, causing distress and struggle within oneself, when help can be received in a much faster way.

Your farmers learnt how to cultivate wheat, and then grind wheat, and make wheat into bread, and they spent hours and hours doing this thing, when there was an apple tree nearby.

It was unnecessary to grind the wheat for nourishment as they could have sat in the **bliss** of abundant existence in the shade of the tree.

Your well-being does not require toil, it does not require sweat, it does not require tears. In fact, toil, sweat and tears are the opposite of your well being.

You are where you need to be, and the only reason why you would need to have toil or sweat or tears, is because you do not appreciate where you already are. It would mean that you believed somehow to know better than the All-That-Is for placing you where you are. Do you know better than the plan that put you where you are? Do you know better than the situations, and the circumstances that put you where you are? Are you trying to get to some place you are not? Why would you need to be some place that you are not? Reflecting upon this question will expose to you, beliefs that perhaps you are ready to let go. At any time that your mind is telling you that you need to do something, we would suggest you take a pause and ask why it is you need to do anything at all? For there is no need for anything, even when it is the mind itself that is demanding that from you.

If you are not able to go, what you call 'deeper into

FROM STRIVING TO SURRENDER

service' at this point, it is simply because this is what is serving you the most at this point in time.

It may be because you are wanting to face the struggle of desiring something that does not arrive immediately. It may be because there is some other focus that is pressing upon you, asking to be resolved before you commit yourself 100% to this direction. Perhaps you are wanting to learn the art of being okay with how things are at the moment. This would involve accepting that things are exactly as they are at this time and that even with your desire for it to be different, it is perfect.

You can relax. There is no urgency. Your skills and existence are exactly as they need to be in this particular field at this time. It is safe to let go of any form of control in this situation. The discomforts that you're feeling now will not be there for long.

Expect the unexpected.

The mind will attempt to fight with the All-That-Is in any way it can to prop up its own importance in the face of the reality of neutrality of all things. So if your body is having a reaction or your heart is communicating with you, telling you in the Now what action to take, your mind often says you need to do something different than what is being felt. The mind, or ego, or separation, does not exist when faced with the light and therefore has a need to argue with the All-That-Is.

You may allow yourself the flexibility of your trees, for you are completely new in every moment and none of what you do has any importance at all. Remember the neutrality that arrives with oneness, with infinity.

Here is the way that nature makes plans: It has its intentions. It sets up the conditions for the results that are desired and then it allows. If conditions change, or intentions change, it is flexible with that, and it adapts.

There is no harm in planting a seed, as long as you are not invested in what grows. It is what you Are, not what you do that determines what your life will be.

Relax into spending each moment knowing you are in service to others. Use your energy to diminish the outlines of where you believe yourself to end and another to begin. Find a way to release your sense of unworthiness and substitute it with an approximation of love with which the Creator sees you already, having created you and use this permission slip to move further in the direction to where you no longer need **permission slips**.

We would like to remind you as well that there is no rush. Many of you, the author/our vessel included, have the **distortion** towards control and speed. Slowing is always a positive choice as rushing implies that you are future oriented, and the future is actually the Now. This misunderstanding that the sooner one completes a task the better one will be can be let go of. There is nowhere to run to, and you cannot know what your actions will lead to, so do not pretend to know.

The only evidence that you have ever had that action causes reaction has been you referencing in the Now something that seemed to have happened in the past but apart from memory you have no proof that something ever did happen.

There is a flexibility in time and space that you will soon - and we laugh because 'soon' is a time based concept and so we can replace the word 'soon' with 'now' - be able to manipulate at will. Nothing has ever happened, and nothing can ever happen. All time and all space flows through you and not the other way around.

We are hoping that these words have given you some relief. We know that you have been thinking that you have been struggling, but you have not, you have simply been in a bath of new energies without knowing you were in the bath. Light yourself some candles, put on some music, and grab the bubbles. You may relax.

We remind you as well that all timing is perfect. Everything is occurring exactly as it needs to for you in this moment in time. If you do not seem to be where you think you should be or doing what you think you should be doing then it is because you are needed in this perfect now moment else-where, and that elsewhere is exactly where you are. Your days are being spent currently exactly as they are meant to being spent. This does not mean you are not in service. You are in service simply by existing.

You do not need to try so hard. You do not need to push so hard because the pushing and trying is toward what you perceive as your best outcome. Your best outcome in the game that you are currently playing is to finally believe you do not know what is best for you. It is full surrender into the faith of the What Is.

You don't need to worry about it. We know you are worthy. You couldn't be here if you weren't. There's a really big bouncer at the door.

You are what is. Surrendering does not mean surrendering to what is external to you. Surrendering is the action of understanding that everything is you.

The reason why the concept of surrender feels foreign or is one of the later steps that one takes is because it is terrifying to think that one may give up that control.

However, when a being comes to a point of there being no more moves to make, surrender is the only option. You are encouraged, over and over, to surrender before that is the case, however it is not entirely possible as this requires you to see that there are no more moves.

The good news is: The moment that it happens you begin to laugh because you realize there was never anything to surrender to or from and this What-Is was you, it is You.

Coming back from surrender with that knowledge means that you can navigate your life with full empowerment and embodiment as you are no longer in a state of separation from anything that is presented to you in this incarnation.

We will say that resistance requires far more energy than releasing does. One does not place an enormous amount of energy into anything if they do not see some sort of benefit in it. It is not an accident to place much energy into something and therefore resistance and maintaining this resistance is something in which you are invested.

There is some fear of pain that will be released when you let go of this striving and resistance to surrender. Fear is the motivating energy required to maintain this block. If you are able to individuate the specific fear, you will be able to face that fear and let go of the resistance. If you were to see how much power, effort and force you are using to maintain that block, you would have a slight idea of how powerful you actually are.

You will have moments, of course, of confusion after this point as well. It is normal. It is part of what helps you to do that process over and over again. It is cyclical.

But they are not opposing: Surrender and the fact that it is all in your control. They are the same thing.

Another common experience when attempting to be of service is defaulting to patterns of the sensations of guilt or shame.

We will not even call them emotions. Guilt is not an emotion. Shame is not an emotion and blame is not an emotion. They are simply erroneous perceptions of a situation. They are thoughts that cause emotions, but they in themselves are not emotions.

We will state that the only reason why these sensations could be beneficial would be because they can show you that they are not beneficial.

When beings remember that they actually cannot harm one another and it is only one's own perceptions of a situation that cause suffering, there will be levels of freedom in interaction that are far more loving than they are presently in your reality. These thought habits block connection by reinforcing erroneous perceptions of self and other.

There is actually no thing that you can do in existence that would cause guilt. You cannot be guilty of action because guilt requires judgment. And since All-That-Is is accepted by All-That-Is, any form of judgment is in dissonance with truth. The moment there is dissonance with truth there will, fortunately, be emotions that let you know that you are not in alignment with truth.

If every time the sensation or perception of guilt arises you were to reiterate that you are perfectly innocent and that your actions are God moving through you and teaching through you, you would immediately feel relief.

Shame is similar. Shame means you believe that something you have done or something that you fundamentally are, is not acceptable in the eyes of God or All-That-Is.

Of course you're going to get a tap on the shoulder from the 'big guy' asking: 'What are you thinking? How is this possible? You are so amazing and special that you have done something that I could possibly not approve of? You have done something outside of my realm? How?'

Allowing yourself to let go of the thought habits of shame, blame and guilt, even if it the only thing you accomplish in this incarnation, is enough service for your entire lifetime.

lthough channeling has gained popularity in the past several decades there still remains a strong stigma surrounding it. Most are confused about what it means to channel in general and especially in regards to channeling an external consciousness in the way that I do in relation to Vagrein. Sometimes there can be a superfluous glamorization of channeling or channeled content that is biased and unbalanced - placing the material on a pedestal without discernment as to whether or not the content resonates. Other times people can disregard it completely due to skepticism or the beliefs that it is impossible to channel and that the channeler is a charlatan - in this way they miss out completely on its potentially beneficial messages. I, myself have made both of these errors in the past by giving channeled content both too much and too little attention.

Since the dawn of recorded history, channels and prophets have been worshiped, revered, feared or burnt at the stake - all depending on the fashion of the times. None of these actions make capital, in a holistic manner, of channeling's full capacity to be of service to humankind.

I am lucky enough to be in a time-space where I am extremely free to experiment with my gifts and distribute Vagrein's message without hindrance. I am also ever-grateful to you, the reader, for taking an interest in this new era of information and approaching it with such open hearts and minds.

Vagrein will now explain more clearly how it is not only people like me but all of us, that are channeling, all the time. Although now it may still seem like there is something different about what I do, it is completely unremarkable and simply an ability that we all have. I happened to have honed it, quite accidentally, in a certain direction. Everyone has the potential to channel what seems like external wisdom and have direct access it for themselves. Beyond that, anyone has the capability to access the entire content of the multiverse and bring it to physical reality in any number of expressions and forms. By knowing your potential these skills can be augmented simply by tuning into the frequencies you want to see more of on the planet.

Everything is channeling because nothing comes from physical reality. Everything is channeling because everything arises through con-

EVERYTHING IS CHANNELING

sciousness.

For matter to exist it must arise through consciousness. For conscious-ness to be connected to matter a channel is needed. Channeling is the act of connecting consciousness to creation.

The physical body is a piece of technology. It is the equivalent of your mobile phones. Your phone would be completely useless if it was not connected to anything. You would not be able to make any calls in or out, you would not be able to use or have access to any of the information that you so easily have access to at this time.

Your body is your personal mobile phone connected to the network of consciousness. In exactly the same way that you do not see the data until it is appearing upon your screen even if it is constantly coming through the airwaves, your **soul stream** is not visible until it is arriving within your physical vessel.

Then it is able to be communicated into your physical reality through your choice of expression. Not seeing it does not mean that it is not there. It also does not mean that if your phone were destroyed, suddenly the Internet would be destroyed with it. All the data that was being streamed to your phone before its destruction would still exist and all you would need to do it buy a new phone, put in your password and you would be instantly reconnected.

This is exactly the way that human incarnation and **reincarnation** works. Your bodies and your personalities are simply the actual physical gadget and the interface through which the technology is accessing to the information.

Channeling is the energetic aspect of that connection. You can think of different types of channeling as different software or apps installed on the device.

Up until recently, humans only had the ability to make standard telephone calls. Suddenly the Internet was introduced and there is multitudes of information available at the touch of a button.

This is what is currently happening to humans on your planet and why many of you will have access to seemingly other forms of consciousness in similar ways that our author does.

From previously being able to only place and receive calls, you are now beginning to access all the data that is available in the vastness of conscious-ness.

Your bodies are, at this moment, being upgraded to be able to handle all that data. It is as if you are installing new applications. This is why many of your are feeling tired. It is a systems update. However, if you never choose to open those new applications to see what new functions and data are available to you, you will not be able to take advantage of the fact you now have access to all of this extra information and ability.

Humanity has had access to more of the etheric realms than your other species for ages. Art, music, movement and mathematics are all examples of channeled materials which you are accustomed to all having access to. The only difference between new forms of channeling which seem external to you and those with which you are accustomed is the amount of perceived time that they have been in your field and the faculties with which you receive them.

Everything you do and everything you are is channeled from consciousness. Channeling is the function of being within existence and allowing 100% whatever is in the What-Is to come through your individuated being without any form of resistance added by the mental plane. Any time you are being 100% surrendered, you are 100% channeling **Source Energy**. It comes in infinite different formats and indeed, even when you are proposing resistance you are channeling.

Channeling is any expression that is not based on your understanding of the functionality of matter. It is expression that arises without you thinking that you know. This means that all internal information and experience is channeling. It is the stream that connects the physical world of the sharing of thought and knowing to thought and knowing itself. It is how consciousness, source, life and existence enter into matter.

All expressions of matter within your physical plane are channeled form. Without a channel connected to source there would not be the ability to navigate the physical realm in the way that you do. Matter cannot function without essence infused within it and the action of channeling is what infuses and connects these two inseparable ideas.

It is because they are inseparable that channeling is a universal principle, accessible and being accessed by all. It is likewise inseparable from you. The very act of being animate is channeling.

Even an inanimate object, a rock for example, is channeling its essence, it's stillness, the molecules that make up its form and the wherewithal to remain in its physical configuration from source.

Channeling is the slowing of energy into form.

Human beings are in a constant state of channeling - unconscious and conscious. An example of unconscious channeling will be your natural ability to maintain form. The energy that composes your physical boundaries is channeled by you from Source in a way that keeps your skin from dispersing into the atmosphere. Without access to the infinite intelligence that keeps matter within its principles the physical would dissolve back into the non-physical. It is also the principle by which your heart knows to beat and circulate blood throughout your bodies.

Other channeling you are unaware of performing on a constant basis are your thoughts themselves. You are, in every moment plucking from the sea of consciousness which thoughts to allow into your awareness.

Everything you believe to be 'you', your personality, preferences, desires, talents and dreams can be categorized as channeling. The question is are you channeling consciously the elements of which you have conscious control? Or are you allowing for what comes through you to be random, disorganized and chaotic simply because you have been unaware that you have the option to choose?

You have access to all of consciousness and now that you are aware of such, will you choose to call in more or less of what you are currently allowing to pass through you in your daily experiences?

Channeling 'External' Entities

Channeling in the form of a human who has stepped off the controls of their physical vehicle temporarily to let another energy through is no different from what we are proposing are your everyday forms of channeling in that it requires no specific set of skills. Passing through the vessel/our narrator is still simply source energy and is still made up of the same consciousness. When a human decides to listen to internal inspiration to take on the role of channeler it is no different than their inspiration to express their favorite flavor of ice cream or smile at a stranger. They are deciding to exercise and strengthen a muscle that is available to all of you in the same way an athlete chooses to train muscles that are available to all of you.

The runner trains for speed. They train for strength and endurance. On race day they are then able to successfully run the races with what seems to be superhuman capacity. While the possibility to be a runner on a competitive or professional level is not available to all, even with the highest levels of training, because of genetic predisposition, those who do realize this predisposition and follow the call to train in this way are not in any way superhuman. Every one of you, bar some exception, is born with the eventual capacity to run and given the right circumstances, such as being chased by a tiger, would.

You may view one who channels external aspects of consciousness as one who has chosen to allow another element of existence to drive the vehicle of their bodies for a moment. It is as if they have chosen to sit in the passenger seat or the back seat of their car - being their physical incarnation - to allow for source energy to come or through them. In essence they have opened the driver door of the car handing over the keys and put themselves in the back of the car to relax and see where they will be taken to. Later, they switch back to the driver's seat and resume their current life experience.

In the same way that the runner does not run to every meeting that they have at the speed that they are capable of on the track, one who is channeling does not position themselves in the passenger seat of their car during their daily experience. As the athlete trains muscle, channels train space. As the athlete works towards endurance, the channel relaxes into surrender and allowance. Then, depending upon the tone of the muscle of the channel, results will be seen.

The major part of you too, as an individuation, is non-physical with a primary channel connecting to your body from source. Everyday upon waking you naturally begin to channel and reconnect to the same personality that you did yesterday. It is so customary for you that you are not even aware that you are doing it. Your spirit is not housed in your body in the way that you would imagine it to be. Channeling external entities is simply becoming aware of what you do most regularly and choosing to bring in an energy with which you do not personally identify. Each of you has the capacity to re-position your consciousness to use your body and mind to access or allow seemingly different portions of consciousness.

All versions of all beings are parallel versions of one being.

When channeling, you are connected to your parallel versions. The

---

4 Even if it may seem one is channeling and external aspect of consciousness or separate element of existence it is not truly the case. All is One and so a channel is simply accessing more of themselves and all of which they do not normally have conscious access.

specificity of a parallel version with which one can connect, will depend on the decisions and free will of the channel them-self and this, in turn, means that with enough awareness of one's free will and preference all parallel versions are available, including those which, from a non neutral perspective one has put on a pedestal.

You can as easily tap into the consciousness of **MacGyver** as **Jesus**.

DIFFERENT SOURCES HAVE DIFFERENT MESSAGES

Some question all the different channeling sources coming from different schools of thought. This can be answered by looking at your personal intention to hear conflicting messages. The confusion that you have chosen in this experience be a permission slip to continue your doubt and experiment with solidifying your own **intuition**.

Collectively, **co-creation** involves not only the beings in your matrix but all the beings outside of it and the selective call of the beings in your matrix of this type of communication and their own personal desires and intentions. And so you will have beings who in their chosen learning on the planet will have a need for what you call the empowerment teachings for they are on a lesson plan of learning that they may create their own reality. Which is a lesson that is overdue on this planet.

There are others who have come to learn the lesson of letting go. They will attract the channels that have this message for them. They will not hear the other channels or they will hear them at the amount that is necessary for them to have their lesson as well as sub-lessons. What is useful to understand and remember is that lessons are not contradictory. Channeled material does ultimately come from the same source as you do.

You can go to a butcher shop and Phil will cut you a piece of meat. When you return the next week and find Sharon, she may cut you a different piece of meat. This meat may not be to your preference. You will have different messages from different channels because they are, in their way, individual as well. So Sharon or Phil are the same as Abraham Hicks or **Edgar Cayce**. Everyone cuts the meat differently because there is a desire from their clients for the meat to be cut in that way.

When you hear different messages it is because you are going to different butchers. It is possible that you do not yet have a preference for how your meat is cut. In this way you get to taste many different cuts. It does not devalue any of the cuts of meat but you get to choose what you prefer and as you do you will find that the messages get more and more similar. You will say to myself "I don't understand why everyone is saying the same thing" because suddenly they will be.

INTUITION IS CHANNELING

When you have an inspiration, you are not having an inspiration about the future but about the present. You are tapping into a possibility of the What-Is, in the what is Now because What-Is is the complete manifestation of the thought. So, you can begin to think of your inspirations as doors that are opening with invitations to pass through them and every invitation will lead you to another room.

With these invitations lining up one after another, perhaps even in different directions, you can begin to feel they lead to different things for yourself and for others.

There is nothing you 'should' do, in all of creation. Creation does not ask anything of you, it does not put obligations upon you. It does not believe you are better or worse for having taken an invitation or not taken an invitation. There is no level of merit in all of creation, but the invitations are there for you to play the game of deciding.

There is no consequence in not following the inspiration. Except for the one you are putting on yourself. We assure you that the moment that you allow yourself to say no to an invitation you will still be presented with more invitations. For that is another lesson to learn. There is no end of inspiration, there is nothing that needs to be grabbed, or held onto or forced. The direction is flowing downstream, is often the most delightful way to go.

Many of you reading this, if not all of you, are in touch with so much inspiration and the belief that something needs to be done with them but there is nothing that you can miss that you were not meant to miss because there is always something even more wonderful waiting for you. The fear that you may have about not grabbing hold of these invitations and not acting upon them is only there because you haven't had the right invitation yet. The one that screams to you that you can't even sleep at night. And it will come. You will get so many more inspirations.

CREATIVITY IS CHANNELING

Art in any form is always a co-collaboration with the collective conscious-ness. The creative spark is universal. The desire to use any form of creation in order to bring joy and light to another being is service no matter if that is of a quality that one deems worthy of merits or beauty. That creative spark, the intention that flows while the artist is creating, is the gift that one then can impregnate their work with and pass on to the potential viewer, or listener in the case of music.

Whether your artwork comes from what you are imagining, or sensing, or experiencing as an external, or esoteric source or whether it comes from your own personal light, it is of equal value. It has equal power for the people you are serving with it.

Just start. Just experiment. You can be less critical of yourself in the results of this creativity. You are a creator. You are creating at all times. If this creativity needs to flow in a certain direction in a certain way we would suggest just take any form of creativity and begin to create with it. Often many of you are skilled in writing. It is part of your culture to learn how to write when you are young and so we would suggest in that case that you could spend some time writing just without thinking in the mornings as you are fresh to the day. If it is more of a visual arts type of creativity you could do the same. Just pick up any form of creating tool and play with it. If the creativity is more of a project based or an entrepreneurship type of system for you it does not matter what you think you need to do or what you think you should do.

What you could do is to start playing and see this as a game. It is.

The joy that will come with that will naturally build pressure up behind the blockage and you may find yourself in a situation where suddenly you are overcome by emotion that is not likened to joy. Perhaps sadness, perhaps anger, perhaps disgust or any other type of emotion where one normally sees negative however we would suggest to you that when this does happen to allow it for that is the blockage to be removed, and then the joy and the creativity and the inspiration will flow freely through you.

Isn't All This Just Crazy?

We would prefer to discuss this via the word 'insane' as opposed to 'crazy', because the 'insane' points to the lack of health while sane of course is pointing to health.

This question could only arise if one had the fear that their thought patterns, and following intuition and inspiration or accessing channeled materials were unhealthy.

To determine if this were the case one would have to re-frame what they believed was meant by unhealthy. If it is healthy to go along with society as you have known it until now, then please do not do anything based upon your intuition or based upon your heart. These behaviors are not healthy according to the way that your society is currently arranged at the moment. However if you are of the mind that the society in which you live currently is actually not doing very well and is actually not very healthy, then perhaps this new way of living and being is not insane. Perhaps it is the concept of insanity that is insane.

We would say that you will be able to know what is healthy or unhealthy, dangerous or not dangerous based upon how it feels. If something feels positive there is a very good chance that it is. If something feels negative we would say to distance yourself from those thoughts and from those actions. You are in a position where you can learn to trust yourself and your intuition and perhaps if at times you find you make some unusual decisions they are there to lead you towards more faith at this time. For if your intuition told you do the same things that you had been doing normally you would not develop faith. You would just develop more of what you had normally been doing.

If the actions that are coming from your intuition are not harming yourself or others the worst that could happen is someone thinks you are a bit odd. Or they do think you are crazy. Perhaps then your intuition is leading you to these strange behaviors to overcome this fear.

A Desire to Channel the Non-Physical

You may believe that you would like to become a channel of non-physical entities, but this can only be because you are not understanding the significance of your own natural form of channeling that is currently arising within you. You are already a channel. If an entity or entity group is paired with you to bring information to who would hear it, you will know this exactly when you are meant to know and it will be a natural progression to that end. You cannot create this from a state of wanting it because the wanting it itself is distorted. To want this connection is to believe that it is significant, which we are endeavoring to explain it is not.

You are an individuation of the whole and therefore bringing forth the information that your current individuation is meant to bring forth at all times.

Perhaps it does not seem that you are channeling external information in the same way as the author of this book, but in many ways, neither is she. There is no difference between internal and external, there is only difference in where you identify the boundaries of the self. If there are no boundaries to self, then everything is internal, including anything from which you would dissociate.

The information that you are channeling, and then identify with as your personality or 'mine' is also not yours as an individual. The intelligence that you channel is simultaneously yours and not yours.

There's no need to desire to be a channel because being a channel means nothing. This intelligence is always available. The only thing that we would advise to desire is to not desire, but not in the way it is commonly explained as if desire is something bad. What you naturally desire is also the desire of the Creator. In the same way that intelligence is both yours and not yours, your desires are both yours and not yours. All.

Any query on how to become a channel comes from a space of wanting to make that yours or of it making you somehow better or that striving will make you somehow better, but you cannot get better than perfection. There is no better than What-Is. An attempt to become better is par with an insult on What-Is. There cannot be any improvement on What-Is and so to look for improvement goes against allowing. To go against allowing is to go against the stream of perfection, intelligence and an energy that wants and desires what you want and desire which is the best outcome for all. The stream desires to flow through you, and does, but you block it by holding, erroneously that same desire.

So to want and allow the best outcome for all one needs to remember not to try to strive for perfection in what perfection already is, and at the same time hold oneself, one's image of oneself with gentleness and compassion in knowing that even the desire to strive for perfection is perfection - and on and on it goes.

Be without judgment.

Your entire system will relax when you are without judgment. When you are as you are; the observer, without layers and layers of memory and judgment applied upon it, you can relax. Your imagined ailments will heal, as attention leaves your physical body. You will be able to see the signs and the clues for direction, if there were to be a direction, and even if you did not see any clues, your direction would be clear.

So you do not need to know how to be a channel. It is clear you are already a channel. You do not need to know what you are channeling. You do not need to know why you are channeling.

Beyond **the veil**, there is no need for communication.

What is known to one is known to all.

The first work necessary to access and become part of this network is to drop the block to it.

It takes far more effort to keep the block in place than to allow it to fall. In fact, allowing it to fall takes no effort. But you are unaware of what 'no effort' looks and feels like.

It is only important to know what would be your motive for that interest. You are already open and understanding the motive will allow you to understand anything that could block you. It is in this that lies the paradox of working on this type of communication because it is only you who could choose not to communicate. That is the choice you're making.

We are looking for more of your kind who are willing to open to our messages, but of course, that only means that you are looking. We see the acceleration that is possible. We see that there are many that share our will which is your will and yet still feel alone in this desire.

The channeling happens whether or not you speak it. You are all sensitive and it is doubt that does not allow you to accept what you and we are giving to you. It is not that we are giving to you, it is that you are coming to the space in which all is offered and you are selecting what to pull down into your experience. From this perspective you may understand that we do not have any separation from you and the many flavors of what you would call non-physical entities perhaps. It is actually all the same consciousness as there is only one consciousness.

If your desire remains verbally channeling, you must have the courage to vocalize any words that come into your mind. This vessel always judges our first statements as ridiculous and always says 'No' before she says 'Yes'. We have to repeat the first sentence many times before she will say it, and then she does, and there is just flow. So to channel in this way means to feel ridiculous, and do it anyway. This vessel has made peace with how ridiculous she is and we thank her.

It is an assumption that the ability to channel verbally happened quickly for her. It has taken 20 or so years. But as a river can build up pressure behind a dam for a very long time, a dam will eventually, if not maintained, crack and break. Then the river will flow at its full force in the path of least resistance.

It is possible that if you can feel you are indeed meant to channel that you have a similar dam that is currently in the cracking phases. It is possible that a dam wants to be dismantled by you manually or it is possible that the river will eventually find its way to break through any resistance that still remains.

In the case of this vessel there was a moment of letting go of the maintenance of the dam in any way whatsoever and enough pressure had built behind it that the transition seemed seamless.

The truth is that we are always speaking with all of you and there are those of you who are more or less skilled at maintaining blocks to us. Consciousness is all one and so there's not one of you who is not connected to all of it, all of us, all of you, all of each other. It is just that you believe that you are not. If your desire is to come to a space where communication and this form of energy flows through you more freely look at the beliefs that you have currently why it is not or they are not.

When you are installing a new program you have the option of having a walk-through where tools are pointed out to you and you experiment with the tools following simple instructions, in order to understand how the tools work for you to be able to be more creative further down the line. With this form of communication the program was installed on both ends and the tools were being experimented with on both ends. Your host, the vessel, has had a period of adjustments and we have had a period of adjustment and you with whom we are communicating have had a period of adjustments in which we have all gotten to know more or less the basics of this new form of rendezvous.

The ability to connect to any entities that you may perceive as separate from you, is directly related to the ability and vicinity of your energy frequencies. Therefore, the ability to connect with an entity is related to the natural, let's say, soul family that you are attached to as you are like branches on the same arm of a tree.

If you would like to take this analogy further you could say that you, as the individuation of you as a human being, are a twig on the branch of that soul group, and it is because the same sap flows through that branch into this twig that you have a direct channel to your shared consciousness which eventually leads into the All-That-Is of the essence of tree-'dom.

If you would like to understand in terms of linear timelines which, of course on the experiential level do exist however on the universal level do not, you may play with the concepts that there is a future version of you or a future version of the entity group that you are channeling that talks back to you through time and space to give you information and wisdom that is not currently accessible by the members of your current space time location.

Yes, in some ways we are a future version if you want to say that, but as there is no linear time we are not the future version we are a present version.

Back to the analogy with the tree; yes there is a trunk and a branch and a twig and a leaf. It is all connected. It does not mean that the branch is more significant than the twig - for it is the twig that does the growing, it is the twig that produces the leaf. So past future higher/lower there is no differentiation in the whole.

We are One. You are One and it is a beautiful exploration to have relationship with, or become aware of, both the individuality of a branch and the oneness of tree.

What seems like a dual thing, two separate aspects of this incarnation, do not in fact hold any form of individualization. What you see as your everyday life and what you see as your separate **multi-dimensional** reality are in fact One. You may think of your everyday life as the dream, in the same way you now think of your multi-dimensional reality as the dream, for in your multi-dimensional reality you are having a dream that you have this strange limited earth life where you have forgotten yourself and in which you struggle to remember, all the while doing the best of your capabilities to serve those around you with this gnawing sensation that something is not quite right. And just as in your reality you remember throughout the day about this dream, in the dream you remember throughout the day about your reality and they are flip-sides to the same coin.

The yin and yang symbol has a point of light in the dark and a point of dark in the light and they intertwine, these two dreams, and in both you have memory of the other, as you are what you imagine to be awake.

Not all who have chose to experience the incarnate self, have another dream space or parallel incarnation as intertwined in this way. If you have chosen this it is because it is that point of access to the dream from each dream that allows information to pass in a particular way between two dimensions. Your human selves are now in the process of opening more of that light point and we are an example what can come through from that dream. Know that this dream is reality in as much as your reality is reality and that the other version of your individuation, dreams of you as you dream of it. Should you allow for that to become a **lucid dream**, your current physical incarnation in this reality, the one that will hear this voice will have access to the information and decision making capabilities, of that individuation of your consciousness, that you are familiar with in the dream state.

It is safe to allow and trust the wisdom that comes through from the multi-dimensional non-physical self as there is a more drawn out perspective on what you would call your life. At some point with surrender, willingness and training the seeming two factions will be able to seamlessly coexist with full consciousness in both realities and in both dream realities.

The true waking state, however, is aware of neither. The alignment of your shared intention is the key to this congruence and unity of experience.

You are wise and know all that we know. It is just a question of remembering to have faith. You have your teachers at the push of a button and us at the distance of a flash of thought. You are supported and cannot fail.

Lean back. Lean into it. It is so beautiful.

 *agrein has discussed relationships between humans many times. They take it as an opportunity to teach unity because any questions of 'how to relate' automatically point to not yet understanding that the way one relates to another is the same way they relate to themselves. The other is the self. Like many of the topics covered by Vagrein, the solutions are blatantly simple. Change the perspective and the answers are already in front of you and crystal clear.*

The relationship with Self, takes precedence and is the cornerstone and foundation of all other relationships. It is also true that all being one, all relationships with other-selves are ultimately likewise the relationship with self.

If one version of you is so complex, and multifaceted, on it's seemingly own, then two or more of you in conjunction have the individual facets that together created a third entity through the interaction - that of the relationship itself. For this reason each relationship is as unique as the parts of it, and every relationship or interaction, is equally formative for both parties.

No matter the circumstance or semblance of a relationship, however casual or serious you attribute it to be, it is fundamental for the story that is developing, which you call your life. Every relationship and situation, and interaction you have with another being, makes your entire life story possible.

The understanding of this will allow you to begin to form the levels of respect and honour for other-selves that will be most beautiful and effective for you as you journey throughout your life. Not only are other-selves You in that they are another portion of the same consciousness in the grand 'We Are One', they are literally a parallel version of you. If time were linear this could be likened to you having already been them in a past life, and they already having been you. The miracle of the two aspects of yourself 'sniffing each other out' in this way is both predestined and determined by your mutual choices of co-creation on a moment to moment basis.

The shift happening in

YOU AS ALL OTHER-SELVES

many of you reading this currently is an end chapter to relationships as you have previously understood them to be.

You are saying goodbye to your personal relationships as you adopt the understanding that truly, this being a **collective**, nothing can be personal.

Ownership and identification within the relationships with the people in your lives or the roles you play in them are coming to an end. Personal relationships are being replaced by awakened interactions that do not see any form of separation between the parties and therefore have only the scope of love and growth. You will continue to be supported or stimulated by those around you and you will always be loved and have an excuse to love, but the specifics of your interactions and those attachments which you now hold fervently will dissolve into the larger bath of your love.

This means, in turn, that the love that you hold for those specific entities/beings will become a more universal love - this is/was your greatest desire - and the benefits of this sensation on a moment to moment basis in your life will be well lived.

You are unaware that you have been living your lives in separation from your Self in the form of what you think are other-selves. You have simply not been seeing that there is another option - the only true option.

In this Now moment you as a collective are feeling the side effects of where you are not fully aligning with the desire to see and love unconditionally. You are in the process of cleaning up the leftover residue of where you have been acting stubborn towards this desire.

Thus far, no matter what teachings you have heard and taught yourselves about unity, the connection of all, and how reality is an illusion, the majority of you are all still very much convinced that you do live within a reality that has certain framing. There is still an element of you that is taking these teachings as figurative as opposed to literal.

When a teacher tells you that time does not exist they are not being metaphorical, they are simply telling you what is true. When a teacher is telling you that All is One they are not being poetic, they are simply telling you what is true.

Separation exists because one believes that it needs to be there. Separation is the result of believing that one is in danger or that there is something that could be threatened. Relationship as you currently know it may seem to be unifying but in fact is a scaffolding propping up the crumbling remains of separation.

Before incarnation, your consciousness is the unified One and as incarnation appears all elements that are seeming separate are regardless connected. The connections with which you have more proximity, as in those personal relationships, are in place because there is a fiber that runs underneath and behind Creation that connects you to that seeming other being is closer than a fiber that connects you to a being with which you have less of a proximity.

The one with which you have less of a proximity does not, nevertheless, become part of a separate creation, they simply are further away from you.

A good analogy for this is a carpet or a tapestry. The threads on a tapestry run above and below the tapestry and there are threads that are next to each other. These threads touch each other. They affect each other. The colour may rub off one onto the other but the threads further away on the tapestry will not be affected by the colour rubbing off from that distant rubbing of the red, let's say, onto the white.

Underneath, on the backside of the tapestry, there is a weaving where one can see that the threads are in fact completely intertwined. They need to be intertwined to create whatever pattern was desired on the front of the tapestry. If they were not they would fall from the hanging and no longer be a part of the creation, and the image of the creation would not be complete.

The same goes for relationships and interactions in your lifetime: You are weaving together with the other threads of which you come into contact. In the tapestry of your life and your life stories it is necessary for you to seem to rub up against the other threads, even though behind the tapestry you are part of the same and cannot be separated.

This may also lend you a perspective on how dear and important and vital to your life every being with which you come into contact is for your particular life story.

Once you can see with such great respect the beautiful nature of the tapestry you are weaving together you will understand that there is the inability for your existence without theirs. The existence and presence of all those with whom you come into contact depends upon your thread holding them into the picture and your existence depends upon their thread holding up yours.

Without a single portion of consciousness, all consciousness would cease to exist. This is a part of the understanding of the oneness of all things.

To this end, it would be wise to stop before each thought, scene change, interaction and action and set an intention or recite a small prayer for the intention to see all as Self and send love to Self through others as you move through your day.

You are in a space where intention creates far faster than words and where you are able to see the material world manifesting before your eyes directly through experience and the mirrored actions of other-self. You are now in a position to prove to yourself the cogs and wheels of the actual fabric of Creation and so these moments of pause and intention will make sure that these gears run smoothly in your chosen direction.

When the energies of love flow through you in powerful ways, allow yourself to focus on the energies themselves as opposed to looking for concrete ways to express the energies. They will amplify, and in their amplification you become their expression.

Those versions of you that you want to share these energies with do not need your specific words or your presence in their physical proximity to feel these amplified energies that flow through you, nor do you need to express to them with words or your physical presence in order to feel the energies. With the increase in generalized love highlighting your system, you will naturally know what action to take to match the love energy and then express in whatever way is flowing. Then these energies will be received in a completely different optic.

The knowing of things not being causal allows you to become the cause.

Once one realizes that both Creation as well as their individual perspective of consciousness, are All-That-Is and simultaneously one drop in the collective perspectives and timelines in all parallel realities and existences - and that one is the only being that could possibly ever have their current experience in the concurrence of infinite other beings - and when the understanding that one's perspective is the **only** perspective that is possible becomes applied on a visceral level, embedded in the cells of one's bodies and being - one can come to understand that this conversation, this text, does not truly exist.

You are creating it in the moment you read it and in the moment it was written and in the moment it was printed on this page. There is only the Now and all of Creation occurs in the Now.

Ask yourself: Why are you creating it? You are able to create it to be anything that you would want it to be. You are awake in the lucid dream. The only dream.

Oneness is the only understanding that can follow this awakening for you have created anything and everything that there is. No hatred would be possible for any of your creation. So the starving children, the ritual human sacrifice, all of the things that you have read about, seen on TV and anything that you have heard about - the crimes as well as every joy and every butterfly - are your creation.

If you investigate it as your creation and look deep into why you have created any of these things you will realize you have created them for yourself to wake up not **from** crimes, not **from** evil, not **from** separation, but **to** yourself. For without the contrast, without these things that do not fit your preference, without these things that underline separation to you, without these things that you see man propose against man, you would never have stopped to look at it with such a magnifying glass.

On a personal level there is of course competition, jealousy, believing that one is talking with another when talking with an other-self - all these things cause or amplify a belief in separation that already lies within you.

The moment you separate yourself from another human being you are separating yourself from all of existence. You are separating yourself from God.

We are not saying 'Go and embrace every other human being', for they are all simply story lines and code arranged in a certain manner to lead you to the next big reveal. You may discern what is applicable to you in your life at this time.

We do not say 'roll over, stop loving yourself and let yourself be walked upon' for who would be walking upon you? Believing yourself to be a victim would be an amplification of separation as well.

Unity or oneness is: "Love thy neighbor as thyself.'" but the word 'as' is irrelevant.

Just: 'Love thy neighbor/thyself.'

'As' implies that there is or could be separation: 'As if they were' thyself. There is no 'as if'. They simply are. They are you. They are simply another version of you.

They are all you. We are all you.

---

1   King James Bible (2017). King James Bible Online. https:www.kingjamesbibleonline.org/ (Original work published 1769), leviticus 19:18

It is always funny when this conversation arises: The many individuations reading these words are very aware of the other individuations and they ask: "If I'm creating these words then what about that other person? Do they have the same experience?"

No. They don't have the same experience. They don't exist separate of you. We don't exist. And ultimately you, as a separate element, don't exist either!

But for this play, we do.

What we would like for you, and what you would like for you or you would not be writing and reading these words, would be to remove yourself from the play so that you can actually play in it.

If you could imagine the freedom that you would have if you allowed yourself to actually believe everything you've heard in these lines.

You would be what you are; which is infinite.

You would be what you are; which is omnipotent.

You would be what you are; which is free.

It all comes from knowing your Oneness. Knowing What-Is.

We see the value of the interaction between beings as one of the lessons you desire to learn and encapsulate at this time. Love and Unity.

In bumping into each other you have the opportunity to tweak your understanding of these concepts in a way that you would not if you understood completely you were alone, all one. When this realization dawns on you all relationships will cease. In the meantime you seem to be having fun doing it so we encourage the continuation of this practice until it has full-filled its service in teaching you that this practice is no longer necessary.

In this illusion of separation, before your journey began here on Earth, every being that you now encounter is/was your closest family on an energetic level. It could not be more intimate.

These beings, every single one of them, is a unique portion of the same branch of consciousness that you have chosen to experience. Even the simple fact that you have decided to incarnate as human and these portions of consciousness which you interact with as other humans have chosen to participate in this dance with you, makes each and every one of them so unbelievably precious.

You have access to ones who are so like you, reflecting you in every moment. You have soul mates and kindred spirits and twin flames and cosmic families but you are not understanding how precious every single encounter you have is, how every hair, on every arm of every being that you encounter has been placed there just for you to experience.

There will be beings in your field that you will give more significance to which will affect you more closely. You will have responses to them on an emotional or physical level and of course you may pursue any of those and you will learn much from the relationships you enter with them. But there are also these subtle relationships and your own influence upon those subtle relationships that are equally essential to your complete complex life story.

Consider a woman in a checkout line at a grocery store, you see her everyday and she sees you everyday but you do not really see each other.

Again, we do not mean that you have to get into deep relationship with every being but we do mean that every being has the potential and is placed in your field for you to be able to learn from them what it is you came to learn from them specifically.

The other-self that you have created in your consciousness to show you more of yourself is created by you, for you and every conversation or interaction you have with that other-self is created by you for you. Remember that you cannot actually interact with an other-self because an other-self does not actually exist apart from you - What you interact with is your own perceptions of the other-self. They do not exist beyond your perception of them and you do not exist beyond their perception of you. This second part is not necessary to our discourse as their perception of you does not exist without your perception of their perception of you.

You are one with all other beings because you cannot separate them from your own perception of them. Try to think of an other-self without thinking of them. Try to see someone else without seeing them. Try to push something away from yourself without perceiving it and therefore making it a part of your experience and therefore a part of you. It is not possible.

Arrive at the understanding that the perception of the other IS the other. Your perception has more to do with you than it does with an other-self. Your perception of the other is all that exists and you feel separate from it, but it is yours. What you are really telling yourself and teaching yourself with this sensation of separation or loneliness is that you feel separate from yourself.

You can control your perception of all that you experience and therein lies the key to controlling and creating your entire reality. It is all lessons. It is all beautiful. It is all perfect and that it is all created by you for you.

Understanding of oneness allows you to exit the mental loop created by the understanding that nothing exists beyond your perception of it.

As consciousness is all one and as we are all one there is no violation on any level of using any other-self in together learning one's chosen lessons because of the contract that one enters into with every other-self. The moment you can perceive another portion of consciousness within your consciousness it has already been agreed upon by both portions of consciousness which, on the higher level of course, are one.

The beauty that arrives from this form of realization is so overwhelmingly potent that it needs to be fed to your being in doses and repetition for if you were to see it all at once, you would be blinded by it.

You are not separate and you are never alone.

It is our excitement that in your present Now there will become times of experimentation with this concept more fully and each of you will wake to realize quite how connected you are and that these connections do not have meaning in the way you have believed connections to have in the past but have completely different meanings and a potency that will skyrocket each of you to your ideal true self.

We see you as the flames of candles, each believing itself to be in the darkness and standing alone. And we see how simple it would be if all these candles were to lie down. We see how much light would be generated by the unified fire that is created. We wish, so much, for you to see the light in one another and see how this burning is communal and how even those that you do not agree with, fundamentally and ultimately want exactly what you want.

It is a word that is so misused and misunderstood in all of your languages, but, love truly is the answer to all questions.

What you believe about the term 'unconditional love' may be different than what we intend by that term. Our intention of that term would require nothing. In fact, requiring something would negate it.

Unconditional love is 'the absorption of other as self without seeing.' It does not require anything to change because there is no judgment. Without seeing, there is nothing to notice to change and, therefore, nothing that stops the perfectly united energy of love. This is the What-Is. In a way, it would mean simultaneously walking away and walking towards. It is in stillness that love thrives.

Unconditional love is possible when one sees very clearly how the conditions we place upon another are conditions we place upon ourselves.

In the understanding that there is nothing to forgive or change, because nothing was ever wrong, one arrives at an opening to that frequency and the ability to feel it in their core.

It cannot be forced.

You cannot want to love something unconditionally and then ask yourself "Why can't I love this thing unconditionally?" because then you are not loving yourself unconditionally.

For some, a stimulus will be external and for some it will be internal but unconditional love does not relate to one or a couple of people. It is something you allow yourself into and you trust yourself into and you love yourself into, and you will know that when you love yourself unconditionally unconditional love will be the only way you see, or rather, do not see, the world that you currently know.

Unconditional love will be who you are because it already is who you are.

UNCONDITIONAL LOVE

Because the full realization of oneness has not been achieved by most, Vagrein continues to meet questions in the space from which they are asked. This chapter answers questions on the specifics of relating within the 'human experience'. As you read this chapter and learn from its wisdom please remember the undercurrent of the broader teachings of Oneness explained in the previous chapter. In this way you will have both applicable knowledge for your day-to-day interactions as well as transcendental knowing that rises above any circumstance and situation that may arise. In time and with practice of the shifting of perspective from separation to unity, you will understand how any of the pointers here in this chapter become redundant.

NEXT GENERATION GUARDIANS

Vagrein often discusses parenting and interaction with children and has pointed to it being a fundamental aspect in leading our race towards the future realities that we prefer.

Your children are not your own. Stop seeing them and treating them as such. They have nothing to do with you. You are not a 'parent'[1]. They are not your child. You did not bring them forth. They came through you of their own will.

You have no responsibility for them other than the agreement you made with them in this collective to make sure that their physical vessels reach their desired maturity. There is very little need of a child for a parent. Perhaps this is quite terrifying for parents who have assumed the current collective understanding of parenting. The main need for a child from a parent or any adult is to protect their physical form for as long as is necessary before their own cognitive ability to protect their physical form comes into play which is relatively early and quite a lot earlier than you believe.

Any other need of a child is the same need that all of your beings have. It is not age specific. All beings have a need

---

1   from Latin 'parentem, accusative of parens ("parent"), present participle of parere ("to breed, bring forth")

MORE ON
RELATING

and desire to be seen, and accepted, and loved - as is.

It is actually the construct that you have of parent-child relationships that can impede this. The rapid evolution of a child in the eyes of its primary caregiver causes distortion between seeing the child as it is in this moment and how they seemed to be last week or how they were ten minutes ago or how they were a second ago.

It is extremely difficult for adults interacting with children to see them as they are in the moment. This is the most important thing that one can do when relating to children because a child , specifically and more so than an adult, is never, even on a cellular level, the same as it was five minutes earlier.

The main developmental initiative of a child is change. Any parent would do well to truly focus their attention, in a form of waking meditation, only on the changing factors of their child. The beautiful thing for the adults around the child is to realize and really soak in the experience of the impermanence of anything. Children remind you of your impermanence.

It is interesting that most adults do not remember having been a child and when they see a child do not remember that they too are, as all timelines are simultaneous, that child.

'Child' is simply a term that you have given to these beings who are newer to this planetary existence than you are.

It is unusually difficult for just one or two beings to believe themselves to be so fully responsible for other beings. It is also unusual that there is no, or very little, concrete and healthy acknowledgment of the role of these guardians in your society. This role is fundamental in that the guardian must endeavor to remain out of the way of the growing child in a state of detached interest, observing the changes and attempting to ensuring that while protecting the physical vessel the being does not take on conditioning that would lead it away from its true divine nature.

Of course in your current configuration of society this is near-impossible so we suggest instead to have much compassion for oneself if this conditioning does occur despite your best intentions. You are still in a space-time where the conditioning and ensuing **catalyst** is necessary for you all to be learning the lessons that you are choosing for your own expansion as a collective.

This guardianship can be seen as the highest form of service to another being that there is. It is common in your society, only because of how it is distorted and arranged, to disregard or diminish this role.

When a being in the role of guardian has a desire to be in service and then is told that the role of parenting is not as valuable as some other forms of service it is extremely damaging and simply untrue.

Your society and world would move in the exact directions you are claiming to want with the simple move of supporting the guardians to support the healthy un-manipulated growth of the young saplings. Much would be resolved in as little as 13 years.

There is a special bond between child and mother as they have shared the same physical vehicle. We have talked about how your soul streams into your physical vehicle in the past and during the gestation period there is a double[2] transmission. The echoes of the transmission never quite cease for the mother after the birth of the child and as the active role as a mother is temporary, this can at times cause some confusion. The children, while never detached from her as a mother figure, will eventually be at their full development and will not be as easily influenced or reliant. The mother on the other hand may in the time of her role as guardian develop an attachment to the child that causes her to unnecessarily focus more on their soul purpose than her own. It is beautiful and biologically necessary to allow a focus of service to be dedicated to them in the time that they are very impressionable in their formation and vulnerable in their physical form but one must endeavor to not be drawn so into the interaction that one believes they usurp the child's connection to Source or is responsible for it. Parent, guardian or not, your main directive is always your own connection to Source.

That said, every action of love that one provides to a developing mind-body complex that houses an energetic being is affecting and influencing every interaction that that being then has with the rest of humanity for all of their existence. Every single one of you has had the parental guidance or misguidance that has shaped you. It is an extremely important role and in many ways a beautiful exchange for the beings involved.

THE CHILDREN AS TEACHERS

---

2   Or more in the case of multiple pregnancies wherein the mother carries two or more offspring.

These parent-child relationship often exist to resolve any past energetic baggage or hiccups on the part of the parent. A child will come to a family to challenge the distortions that remain in one or both of the parents and provide challenges that they would not otherwise have even had to or been able to face.

It is a mutual contract you have come into contact with them and they are teaching you because you are willing to learn. They are your co-workers for your shared mission. You have the opportunity, if you so choose, to enjoy your relationship with these beings as a learning experience towards love, or any other lesson you see fit. They do not need you to fix them, they are not broken. Leave them be.

The contract you have with your children at this time is perfect for the optimal growth of all parties. One can have the same level of growth with more ease, awareness, presence and joy. Every child is presenting to their parents the opportunity to make different choices than their parents made and parenting is difficult in that you will be presented over and over, throughout this relationship, with the idea that you could somehow take over their Source connection. You cannot.

Your children come through you for a reason. They choose you for a reason. They know what your level of consciousness is before they arrive. They know the evolution that they would bring to you by coming through you, and they knew that they would be a big part of that evolution. They do not question whether or not they have infringed upon your free will.

We will take this moment to remind, that guilt is absolutely unnecessary, in any situation. With regards to the children, although it seems to be the case, you cannot truly infringe on their free will. Every being will find its way to becoming who and what it already is. In this same way every source will find its way to the ocean by becoming a river that flows in this way or that and changes course, as necessary.

This said, your interactions with children is not so much to teach them as it is to teach you. If you are a caregiver in the life of a child and you are abusive to that child there are natural repercussions to that, how you see yourself, how you feel about yourself, the circumstantial aftermath of those actions and so on. The trajectory of the life of both parties is changed infinitely by the decisions made within any form of relating. For this, and because of the seeming imbalance of power in parent-child or adult-child relationship, we suggest extra caution when choosing whether or not to treat a child in any way that one would not want to be treated themselves. Interestingly, in your culture this caution goes unheeded and it is most often the children who are most mistreated in subtle and seemingly acceptable ways as well as the most seemingly horrific ways imaginable. We assure you that these debts do not go unpaid.

THE NEXT GENERATIONS

This, and the coming generations, will have more and more evolved beings incarnating on your planet. A lot of these evolutions will be drastic in some way, others subtle.

These children are not like the ones that came before. It is an assumption. The children do not need you. They are all here to serve. You do not need to fill their heads with lies and illusion. The world you think you are preparing them for does and will not exist so there's no need to prepare them for it. There's no need to learn anything when you have universal knowledge of All. The earth and the Creator provide for them. Their natural propensity for love allows them to be who they are, to see other-selves as they are, they are already the evolved species. It is only you who sees them as not. They are gods amongst you, as you are, but they have not yet forgotten . Teach them to hold onto their knowing --Joy-- and nothing else.

You are past the times of normal. There is no more virtue in your schooling systems. There is nothing left to learn that you can teach to the children. It is their turn to come and teach to you. These beings are arriving now because it is time for your true nature to take over where all the intellectual systems have failed.

The systems you have been currently using for instruction are based on separation and division and what is needed now and for the new earth is inclusion of the innate resources that each being comes to this planet with. The children have everything they already need to know programmed into them before birth and all your instruction is now doing more damage than good. Leave them be.

They are not small adults or working towards becoming an adult - fully whole. They are already fully whole at every stage of their development. They are beings equal to you in every way and superior to you in many ways as well. Physically you are evolving, spiritually you are evolving, mentally you are evolving. These beings that come in, every new generation, every new being is an upgrade. Every new being is something that the completeness of Creation was missing. There's another paradox for you.

Could you imagine that if in the first 18 years of a new job someone talked to you in the way that you talk to children? As if you were incapable of performing your job? And if they continued to tell you that all of the experiences you were having in this new job were to someday 'be fully whole'?

You wouldn't be very pleased with 18 years of that kind of treatment, would you? And yet you all survived that exact treatment. And you are all subjecting these small beings to the same treatment. They are not incompetent. They are fully competent in being who they are exactly in the moment.

If you could interact with children with this level of respect and admiration and knowing and willingness to learn and willingness to observe and be present then much of the conflict or questions around parenting would simply dissolve because there would be no parenting. There would be co-existing with beings who had so much to teach you and who in turn would be willing to accept your service.

The children now, among you, that you may label as challenged or handicapped in some way, are not. They have their own journey and purpose here. You take them to 'experts' and try to use external devices such as pharmaceuticals to make them as 'normal' as they can be, given their so-called challenges, but you do not understand that these challenges are their gifts.

All questions relating to parenting are based in a large proportion on your collective conditioning around this topic, and what you believe a parent and child relationship is already. You believe that parents have responsibility, and yes on certain levels they do, but it is not this ultimate responsibility. The child itself is already a sovereign being and most of the work of a truly advanced guardian is simply getting out of the way and healing whatever the relationship with the child brings up for one to heal.

Nothing ever went wrong in your own past and it is your belief that something went wrong that allows you to believe that something could go wrong. Nothing ever does or could go wrong. And so it is from this perspective that we can say that regardless of how you judge yourself, you, in every moment, are doing everything right.

Forget the labels of the role of parenting, reposition your perspective regarding your responsibilities and begin to enjoy the blessing of love that this unique form of interaction can afford you with more ease and joy. If you need to remember one aspect from what we have taught it would be: Let them be.

THE ROMANTIC RELATIONSHIP

You are already in love with every being you meet, you have just forgotten.

That sensation of being in love, with someone, is not exclusive, it is 'What- Is', and we augur to any of you who are able to come to the full realization of that because your life will evermore be full of ecstasy.

Ownership, particularly in regards to the emoto-physical nature of the romantic relationship is a deep collective form of conditioning which, once resolved will allow you to truly begin to love on far deeper and spiritual levels.

The heart is not exclusive, it is inclusive, therefore any form of exclusivity practiced within relationship is a direct affront to the true nature and expression of the heart. It is also completely governed by the fear of loss or lack.

Your soul contracts can never be broken, and so a fear of losing someone is always unfounded for you are connected, no matter what words are shared or not shared, no matter what space is shared or not shared. Any prevention of the natural movements and expressions of an other-self is the lock on the cage to one's own heart. It would be a beautiful expression of your incarnation to be truly share yourself with the people you love and truly allow the people you love to share themselves with the rest of the world. There is no need for that cage and many of your conflicts and resentments are created by the belief that the cage is protecting you from some unseen enemy. The only thing it is 'protecting' you from is the ability to taste and experience true freedom and love with full respect of your own and other-selves' free will.

Coupling occurs when a soul contract exists that requires more of an

---

3   *Potential future child produced by the coupling.*

physical and intimate proximity. This is also in relation to the desire of a third entity[3] to join the union in the form of reproduction via children. There have been cultures who have properly acknowledged the nature of the stimulus to have relationships that for a time involve only two individuations, however at the moment, on the majority of the planet this is not the current paradigm. As you move, as a collective, to clear the distortion surrounding love and relationships you will see how the two only seem to be directly intertwined. In seeing how they are not, you will alleviate many of the complications and discomfort that has arisen within this misunderstanding.

Labeling of Relationships

Do not get confused by the advent of labels and concepts. These are simply methodologies of understanding based upon an observation that many have had before you. A label or concept must not be confused with that it is attempting to describe or the experience itself. When there is a particularly intense relationship that spans the emotional, physical and spiritual realms you are fast to assign names such as other-half, soul mate, twin flame or more. These exist primarily to discuss the significance or importance of these relationships with others in shorthand so as to be able to have conversations about them however there is no special significance to these relationships in the same way there is no significance to the label itself.

Even labels such as friend, sister, parent, acquaintance create disharmony and limitations to the true expression of a possibility of rapport. One can only assign specialness or significance to a relationship when they are seeking for some level of importance within it. It is true that there are relationships that seem to be more intense than a regular relationship, however, no relationship can be more significant than any other relationship. All of your relationships and interactions are here to teach you something that you have chosen to learn in this lifetime.

Adding romantic and poetic descriptions to a relationship may make it more attractive relationship for those of you who would like to remain poetic and romantic. We are not diminishing the relationship itself by any means. A powerful relationship is always a powerful relationship but one who has not labeled their relationship as such does not make whatever powerful relationships they are in any less significant because of it.

There are no rules, however your civilization has implemented many rules and regulations and suggestions on this particular topic that are absolutely useless. If one were to address their current experience directly and ask themselves what are they trying to learn from the intense or at times complicated nature of a 'special' relationship they would have much more success in dissecting the specific information that is meant for them from the relationship or lack thereof.

The label is a distraction both from the relationship itself, which deserves more honour than it is often given, and from one's own journey towards an understanding of self and other.

ATTRACTION

One is attracted to an other-self for a variety of reasons.

Within the experience of the attraction and consummation of attraction the relies the possibility of moving at a increased pace towards learning a specific lesson. Often your lessons are on unconditional love, or oneness, or acceptance, or non-judgment. Being in relation to another portion of self can provide the most accelerated opportunity to challenge oneself to learn these lessons. It is very useful to have an other-self on which to practice judgment and conditions for without these one could not see what percentage of understanding they have arrived at in what they are wanting to understand. The attraction one has for an other-self is therefore put in place based upon the potential that this other-self has in triggering and stimulating the specific lessons that one wants to learn in relation to other-selves on the discovery towards oneness.

You have also come to earth and created this human experience in order to enjoy drama, some game playing, and fun. During the romantic encounters or attraction or sexual encounters that you have between yourselves you have the added bonus of having this drama and fun and intensity of emotion towards your learning that you would not have if all relationships were platonic.

There are many physical factors that lend to attraction as well. There are biological factors that will draw you towards beings that have the characteristics which specifically attract you because of the potential for the two of you to learn the lessons that you have predestined to learn together. The physical body of each being is chosen to fulfill these contracts.

Attraction is necessary for specific energetic codes which are exchanged th during the act of coupling. These codes are metaphysical artifacts of the agreement that you have with another being, either in this incarnation or parallel versions. These codes, passed physically, aid in the development of your learning process and balancing of your energies.

Whether or not one acts upon their attraction is also part of these contracts. Not all attraction requires what you believe to be conclusion in order to fulfill its purpose. In fact, in many cases it is the non-conclusion of the attraction that leads one to the conclusion of the lesson that is being presented or offered.

A romantic or sexual relationship will never complete you despite what your collective has invented to state the opposite. No one will ever complete you. They can't because you are already complete. There are beings here who will challenge you into learning what you came here to learn on a more intense level than those who are simply passers-by in your life. There are beings who will break your heart but it is because of how much they love you on the level in which you have created that contract. There are those who will show you that you are human. There are those that will remind you that you are God.

It is your choice whether or not you will have these sorts of relationships. They will only arrive to you if it is to show you more of what you are not seeing.

Relationships exist to allow you to see where it is you need to grow or if one has already come to a state of loving oneself that there is no more growth in that direction and one can truly love an other-self. Then two may meet and simply choose to walk side by side.

You get to decide everything. If something is consistently not working in an interaction you may sit with your beloved other-self and come up with a new plan. Or you may also look within yourself and find a way to accept it, or you may look within yourself to find the thing that is being triggered most frequently and find a way to heal it, but there is not ever truly an impasse, there is simply the possibility to take a new direction. If you are in a partnership that you believe that you want to continue and yet you face many challenges it is possible to go in a direction together and come out at the other side as a stronger partnership. There are so many rules in your collective about what partnership is which are not actually conducive at all to partnership.

Our suggestion to you is to always focus first on the relationship with yourself wholeheartedly with that same passion that you have, or would have for an other-self whether currently in romantic partnership or not. Treat yourself in all the ways you would treat that loved other-self. Take that devotion that you would give to that other being and focus it entirely upon yourself. You do not need to renounce the idea of love with other-selves. You will have love with other-selves naturally if you love yourself. Even a chance glance across a busy street can be very romantic.

While you are here, experiment with truly loving one self and one another - for once you come back to Oneness and Creation and the All this form of love for 'other' is no longer possible as there is no 'other' to love. It is separation that allows you to even have someone else to love. It is not true love, it is not the ultimate expression of what love is, but for as long as you are learning from these contracts and from this game, you may enjoy it and have appreciation for all it is bringing to you. Eventually you will understand the beauty of the love beyond it and let it go, melting into the universal love that is truly what you are.

Each and every other is exactly the same, and each and every other is you.

ACTIVITY : SEEING ALL AS SELF

Your brains have the capacity to allow you to see with your physical eyes that there is no separation. If you choose, you can look at your physical self in the mirror, or an other-self and relax.

As you look into the eyes, with time, your brain will release a hormone that allows you to see that there is nothing but self.

This is a natural phenomenon that exists so that humans will recognize their children as part of them and will not harm them in their infancy, if there is not a distortion that allows otherwise.

You can use this biological tool to have a direct experience of the union between beings and as you sense this you may then activate this response when you look at a tree or a table or a book.

Do not fool yourself into thinking that **eye-gazing**, which is what this has been called, has anything to do with the other person. It is simply you realizing that you are the other person. There may be people who you trust more, or are more attracted to or aligned with that stimulate this function quicker for you, but if unity is the end goal, then labeling an other-self as special takes you from your goal as opposed to bringing you towards it.

Practice in whatever way with whomever you choose, but as your practice develops, know that the love you have for one will become the love you have for all - if that is your choice, and if not, there is no problem. You may enjoy your sweetheart.

COMMON UNITY

Here we talk of community, or common unity. Reclaiming this term in its original meaning and understanding what exactly is being asked by co-creation can only benefit you at this time.

The term 'co-creation' can be best described as: Several perspectives uniting in intention and reality presenting the amalgamation of the collection of these intentions.

In group situations, it is wonderful to have communication and shared intentions, however these must arise naturally and cannot be contrived or constructed even via the best intention as the free will of all parties and conflicting intentions would not allow for this to happen.

We would advise continuing the noble voyage towards Self as individuals and shared collective voyage towards Self. Have faith, it is all happening and it starts with you.

For a long time, all of you, had to put your enormous hearts on ice, and had to protect yourself from your own desire because all the evidence around you said it was impossible to remain open.

All those around you said it was not going to happen. "This is how things were and this is how things are, be realistic, grow up. Stop dreaming." and yet, here we are, at a threshold where the sadness you adopted because you believed those words, can be released.

Your faith will make the change that you desire.

You may, lean upon those in who's eyes you can see the remembrance. There is a network and family and web forming of those who are remembering and you are safe to give your heart to those beings.

The game that had been played in your childhood and the game that had been played upon earth for all this time, of reciprocity and conditionality, is no longer relevant to you. There is no more need for reciprocity from your heart to another and in return, for as you give now freely, what you give is automatically returned to you, for you have seen the other-self as Self.

It is more difficult to do this with people who are not yet at the same understanding and so we suggest a experimentation: With those whom you feel closest presently on an energetic level - even if these are not friends, even if these are acquaintances, even if these are people with whom you do not interact physically - feel safe to give them your love energetically. You will see as you practice this that is returned for their love is your love and your love is their love.

Allowing yourself to love freely is the Common Unity.

TEACHER, STUDENT + LEARNING SYSTEMS

There are many sources of information available to you at this time. At this crossroads you have many beings both physical and non-physical who are willing and able to give you direction, however any direction that these beings could give you is not yet your direction, for your direction can only be given to you by yourself.

In any interaction where one delivers help to another both are learning and both are teaching. The person who has applied for the help, teaching, advice or healing asks for only and can receive only what they are ready for.

This does not mean that you have to discount any of the information that they, or we, are giving to you. We are all creations of your conscious-ness, and the advice and/or guidance are suggestions from you to yourself, that you believe you need to make to yourself through an external or seeming external source so as to be able to either negate or accept those pieces of information - trying them on so to speak, for once you have tried these pieces of information on they belong to you. They become like items in your wardrobe - things that you will then feel that you have to wear. In some ways you are window shopping. You are playing a game of dress-up. 'What does this feel like? What does this look like on me?' You also know that soon you will have to make a commitment to what you believe yourself to be. You believe you will have to make a commitment but the commitment is only as such until you make the next choice.

There will be no being - no human being or other being - that will be able to tell you beyond your inner authority what is right for you.

They have never been you.

No matter their expertise, knowledge or clarity of perception that another delivers to you about yourself there is always the possibility that you are the exception in all of the world to any of the rules. How could they know?

You will not get information that is different from the information that you are seeking - no matter the source - as there is only one Source.

One can learn only what they already in part or in entirety know for they would not be able to create the answer in another had they not already known of it.

Student/teacher relationships are of this nature.

The student believes themselves to need the teacher because they are not able, holding their own distortions, to arrive at the same information from their own state of being. The moment that you can hear a teacher's voice in the first place, however, is the moment in which you already know the information that will be passing from what seems like their mind into yours.

You already know what is written on these pages as you are reading them and it is you who created them to be here or you would not be able to perceive of them. You would not be able to receive this message if you did not already know.

In reality, there is no time, and so the moments before and after one receives reflection or advice from an other-self, is equal.

In the entirety of your existence and incarnation you will only ever learn what you already know.

Fortunately, you are an infinite being. Omniscient. Therefore, the question is not "How can I know this thing?" It is "What do I choose to know in this moment?"

The beings that create teachers and learning systems choose to have these experiences because, for now, they believe without these experiences they would not arrive where they want to be on their soul journey.

You have chose the experience of reading this book for the purpose of learning what you will from reading this book. This learning may not even be related to the content herein.

All experience presents itself for the growth of the being. It is that old saying 'When the student is ready the teacher will appear.' This is the case because in the very moment the student is ready, they themselves create the teacher or learning system into their reality.

By allowing growth to happen through the adoption of beliefs from the new teacher or system the being then furthers their understanding and expansion.

One is only taught by a teacher because they are choosing to be taught. One is only activated by their soul family because they are choosing to be activated by their soul family.

There are many other-selves on your planet who do not make this choice and do not expand through teachings and do not get activated by their soul families.

All of the systems and tools and concepts are beautiful as they play their diverse roles in the experience of Creation and they are all necessary, but it is all the same thing.

All appearances have milk that can be drawn from them and this milk can nourish. We are not wanting to remove any form of appreciation or enjoyment of systems that you currently use for your expansion. The systems, teachers and expansive relationships are indeed useful and neces-sary for your chosen path or you would have not created them. We are only wanting to remind you, that it is YOU who creates your chosen path and all that you find upon it.

Teaching, even created by you for you, is a method of bringing under-standing from one state to another and it would be well to never adopt any of them as fact, for there is only One fact.

Adopting a teaching as fact, or any idea or thought as fact, imbues it with importance that it does not naturally hold, being equal in every way to the rest of existence. Adopting a teaching as fact stops the learning and expan-sion process as one is prone to build resistance to All-That-Is offered in expansion beyond the level of one's current understanding.

You may think of any teaching or study as a bridge that brings you along your journey. Cling to the bridge and you will not make it to the other side.

We would also not advise, and yet not find any fault with, any system that provokes feelings that flow in the opposite direction of where you want to be going. We would not condemn these systems. In your movement in an opposing direction of your desires you are being re-guided to what you truly want.

One could, similarly, arrive at the progressions that a system could offer by feeling into the source beyond all systems.

For all has equal value.

All training that you have chosen to participate in is not a new learning process, but an unlearning process. It is a forgetting of what would block you from what you already know.

When you relax into your natural state and allow you will find that you knew already all there was that you believed you needed to learn.

It is related, again, to one's intention. One no longer needs the same forms of permission slips that they originally needed when accessing their own internal knowing.

When one creates for themselves access to a teacher or learning system they have the anticipation, that their questions will be answered. These questions are held in the conscious mind then suddenly become questions that they believe can and will be answered. Therefore, without even having to spend any time with that self-created permission in the form of teacher or system, direct access to the information and the same energy that creates the answers is achieved.

Knowing this allows you to step into a realm where all questions are answered as soon as you decide that there will be an answer to the question.

It is one of the keys.

In a possible past, there was more of a need to ask and have your other-self present back to you an answer. Humanity is now moving to a less dense level of consciousness so there is more probability to directly access answers without having to create another being in front of you.

You can trust your sensations and guidance system. We do not want to tell you what is good for you for only you know what is good for you and you should respect that at all times. If you choose. We know that all are Source and all are connected to Source at all times and so know that it is not possible to disconnect from Source and it is not necessary to effort one's way toward Source as one already is.

It would not be possible for you to have consciousness and be part of Creation if you were not already pure Source energy flowing into a vessel which was then able to animate itself through will. This is good news.

Concepts are never Source. Source is Source. You are Source. You are God-life pulsing through material matter, or the idea matter. You do not need any form of perfection before God loves you. God loves you before you have anything to offer. You are the offering. You are what God has offered. You are what source is offering to existence. You are the gift, you only believe yourself not to be.

Eventually a transition occurs in each student to become themselves a teacher. Wherever you perceive yourself to be in the path of your learning allow yourself fearlessly to teach. You cannot blunder if your intention is pure. None of your discoveries are personal or proprietary. Seeking ends when sharing begins.

As you come to teach other-selves with your own knowing, know that even if one looks to you as a teacher and claims to give away their power or have their power taken from them, these are illusions. The experience of whatever occurs with this displacement of self-sovereignty is pointing that entity back in the direction of their own self sovereignty regardless of the outcome of that interaction or relation. It is arrogant to withhold your knowing in fear of influencing another-self to a direction in which they are not sovereign. It is not possible to know better than another what is best for them. They are creating you and your teaching in their own experience for a purpose that serves them directly.

The beings that your voice is meant to touch in some way and help expand in some way. It will touch and expand them in a way that is applicable for them even if it means them seeing you as somehow superior to them on some level. You cannot protect them from their own distortion in that direction. In fact, the catalyst that you potentially provide for them to be distorted more in that direction is simply revealing to them the distortion that was already there.

Leaders have responsibility, this is true but only in that they have a responsibility to remain integral to themselves with the knowledge that their action does affect others. Not in taking responsibility for what that effect is. Any doubt that you have which tempts you to withhold your teachings from another-self points to a belief that you do not have the best interest of others fundamentally at heart. If you knew that you did, you would be accepting of the fact that in those small few of the 7.8 billion who hear and then understood your message, there may be several who adopt it as dogma and interpret it incorrectly for their own benefit and in their own desired direction of learning.

You have many examples in your history of completely selfless beings who come to teach of unconditional love, peace, Oneness and who's words and image and vision have been twisted and then even millions murdered because of it. Regardless, what would have happened had they not taught? One cannot know. One can know however, in this Now, only the benefits of their teaching as well as the eventual confusions that arose from them.

You were not created and did not create yourself to be a 50% version of yourself for that would equate to only 50% of your energy used, only 50% of your life lived and the other 50% wasted. Do not believe that you can control the outcome of others' experiences of you. They are sovereign and so you can feel free to be as well.

Presently on our planet, the economic system is undergoing a huge change and takes up much time, energy and attention of the collective consciousness. This book would be incomplete if the subject of money was not touched upon in some form. Vagrein has spoken many times, mostly in response to questions, on the topics of finance, wealth and **abundance**. As the sessions that make up this volume were concluded in December of 2019, humanity had not yet entered into the global shift that occurred socio-economically with introduction of the Coronavirus. The information in the transmissions therefore touch on the understanding of finance and our trade systems in a unspecific way in order to maintain the free will and choice of opinions of the participants.

Being non-physical for the most part, the systems of collective exchange are very different for Vagrein. Their energetic collective economy is based much in the same way that energy and resources are distributed in our own bodies:

Your organs and muscles need specific levels of oxygen, enzymes and hormones at different times. These are freely distributed by the balances in place your bodies. In the same way, we distribute resources to the portions of our collective that in any given moment, have need for that resource. We do not hoard in one part some warehouse of resources as we know that this hoarding is not only unnecessary but ultimately damaging to us.

If you did not distribute more oxygen to your brain when in apnea, you would lose consciousness and would not be able to swim to the surface of a body of water in which you have fallen. If adrenaline did not signal you to distribute more blood to your muscles when under chase, you would not escape the lion. If you did not send more energy to your digestive systems after a large meal you would not be able to clear toxins from your system.

Cells, organs and systems are not allowed to die in one part of the body because white blood cells, oxygen and energy are being hoarded only in the hallux.

This is a needs-based economy. It is not rooted in equality, as not all needs of all systems are consistently equal. Instead the body functions with an intuitive system of distribution of resources in a synarchic

ALL THAT GLITTERS

fashion. It is natural and functional.

The financial and social systems you currently uphold on your planet do not function efficiently and cannot be sustained because you do not yet know that you are one body with the planet itself. The optimal functioning of all of your parts is ultimately the only way to prevent or relent death of the entire organism.

It is a waste of your life-energy to spend any time at all doing what is not in your higher calling. You did not come here to 'survive'.

Your invented paper-game of 'money' is one of the least comprehensible systems to us, though we applaud your creativity in contriving of it. To think that a species came to existence with unlimited resources and potential only to invent personal ownership of these resources and trade this fictitious ownership in exchange for fictitious numbers is astounding. This, followed by the system of both physical and mental enslavement in order to achieve a collection of these numbers for maintenance of the illusion that you need these numbers to survive, is fascinating. There is a common belief that there needs to be compromise in order to survive, that you must work in order to get this money that you think you need. There is the belief that work must be suffering or hard or painful.

It is time to let go of these beliefs.

If, however you do insist on continuing to play this game we offer that the best way to arrive at manifesting this paper-money you so prize is by placing one's focus and belief entirely on your higher calling while leaving the survival and sustenance of your physical self to your higher being. You are supported one hundred percent in this. When one is focused on their higher calling they are sending out a message to the universe, the planet, or God - if you would use that term - that they are now aligned with the **synarchy** we spoke of earlier. Then, what is needed is provided in a more fluid way as the request for it arrives more clearly to the source of your existence. Of course this also means living outside of the energy of greed and coming to the understanding that much of what you currently believe to be a need is simply a distraction you hold in place to prevent you from having to address a true need.

The financial system you have agreed upon is in rapid collapse now, though will not easily be eradicated entirely. Through this collapse, you will find safety only in the knowledge that the financial security blanket you were once covering yourself with, was nothing more than a childhood toy.

You were always safe as you slept whether the blanket was in your crib or not even though you cried desperate tears when you believed you lost it or it was misplaced.

This will be a very grand and global challenge for many of you. You will be confronted with a choice, that you have yourself have created, to learn the lesson of the fictitious nature of lack. The numbers are starting to become more transparent and there will be those who continue to hold onto the memory of them instead of shifting to the new systems.

These new systems will be based on light. They will be based on the understanding of how horrifically perilous the old systems were and how your global connection of shared resources is your greatest strength.

Many of you will rise to the challenge and let go of limiting beliefs and many of you will choose to remain with old beliefs and the consequences of that choice. Stay true and unwavering to your choice and choose carefully.

Now, on your planet, more than ever, if you believe that a lack of money will bring hunger, you will be hungry. If you believe that a lack of money will bring danger and physical harm, you will have that reality. If you believe there can be no lack in the universe then your reality will reflect a situation where you will be supported and cared for regardless of the changes ahead.

Please note that this does not signify that if one is hungry it must mean that they have not shifted their beliefs in a significant enough manner. These pointers are for your understanding alone and not a method to use as a magnifying glass as you move through your world. In a healthy body, when a cell is hungry it is not judged, it is simply fed.

You often couple your sensation of lack for not having abundance with your sensation of guilt when you do. On this we would like to remind you that the entire financial system, in the way of which you have it set up on your planet, is a self-created illusion and you have forgotten completely that it is self created and unreal. Both lack and guilt are sensations being created in your **emoto-physical body** based upon a complete illusion.

This is not only in regards to the "illusion of physical matter" - but also on a psychological level.

You have agreed that metal, banged into a certain shape or tree bark or now petroleum goods made into pieces of rectangular fabric with certain drawings upon them mean something. They do not but because you have agreed with each other that they mean something, on a relative level they do.

Abundance is having what you need when you need it. Therefore financial abundance cannot exist because nobody needs little coins and pieces of paper or numbers on a computer screen, ever.

What you need is: Security, although you always have that. Nourishment, although you always have that. Love, but you always have that.

In fact, the things you truly need you already have, in abundance. It is impossible not to have what you need in abundance, but one must realize who they are.

If you arrive at the realization that you are not the body/mind and instead are that unwavering energy animating it all, you realize suddenly that there is nothing of any value that can be bought.

You cannot purchase love. You cannot purchase health. You cannot purchase peace or a pleasurable state of being.

You could argue that you need food and shelter, and we agree, but food and shelter are not dependent upon money. Unless you say they are. Which, as a collective, you have. In reality they depend entirely upon the realization of unity with all. When there is a collective realization of unity there will be no one unfed and no one left to the elements.

There has not been a day of your life, up until this point, where you have not eaten for lack of papers and pieces of metal. If you have not eaten it was not because you did not have food, it was because you did not have someone who did have food choose to break bread with you. Yes, the papers and bits of metal have helped you to exchange your time or services for food which you could then choose to eat with another, but you would find that even without these tokens and symbols, somehow food could find you. There is a currency-less existence possible.

Money in and of itself, dare we say, is useless.

You have this system that continually reinforces how absolutely important and fundamental it is. Why? Ask yourselves: In whose interest is it for you to continue to believe this? Is it in your interest?

We do not mean to vilify money. We do not mean to propose that it is evil or good or that there is any opinion upon it whatsoever. We simply may suggest that you recall it is a game that grown children use to substitute their childhood games.

The concept that it is necessary or that the world economy is somehow important and that it must be maintained is absolutely faulted - if as much focus went into cultivating love and unification and brotherhood as maintaining an economy then money would become absolutely unnecessary and an accumulation of wealth would be seen as a sign of doubt.

If financial wealth comes to you freely because you are following your passion and you are freely sharing this wealth; spending it, generously sharing it, donating it or using it in some way that feels good to you then this is one healthy way to interact with money.

If on the other hand you are constantly seeking it and trying to squirrel it away in a tree then it points to you having a fear that without it somehow something bad could happen to you. If there is the belief that something bad could happen to you then the understanding of who you are may be looked at further to find some relief.

Conditionality - "If/Then"- is always a sign to work more diligently on your faith and understanding of who you are and could be an exercise to sit with oneself and ask "If tomorrow, all of my money disappeared then what do I believe would happen to me?" Find out what that fear is, who holds that fear, and then you can let both of them go.

If you do agree to play the game of money in with the rules currently available you have two options if the game is not going the way you choose:

The first has been already outlined to you here and is to quit the game and no longer play. This is not to say, detach oneself from the material world and become a renunciate, rather it is to understand that one is already detached from the material world.

For example, if you find yourself with what is known as debt and state "I am out. I do not play this game anymore." Then perhaps those who you are playing with will not be pleased with your choice. Instead, you can do this on an energetic level while maintaining your integrity and contracts even if you cannot do it on a material or physical level. Of course you can do so if you so choose, and if you had no fear of the consequences, you may. Debt, as all catalysts, is an opportunity to remain in one's chosen state despite circumstance. As debt is often seen as a negative thing, this would be its purpose.

However think of all your entrepreneurs, and even your governments who accumulate debt and do not bat an eyelid. They have transcended the understanding that it is all just a game. You can never owe anyone anything.

In the end we are talking about apples on trees. The paper and the numbers mean nothing.

The financial system is based upon an exchange of goods and services one for another. Or, it was meant to be. And so someone with a basket of apples could bring them to a market and exchange them for a bucket of milk.

One day that the apple farmer did not have apples so wrote a paper and said "I'm sorry, I do not have apples but would still like a bucket of milk. Do you trust me?" and the cow farmer would say "Yes I do, but could you please write me a reminder?" A piece of paper or a stone would be taken out as a reminder of how many apples were owed to the farmer of the milk.

This is your first example of debt and of money. By this example you see how all of your money is debt. It is someone indebted to you. You are all exchanging debt.

Every banknote you have is, in theory, a representation of apples; the first apple[1].

You are trading notes that say "I owe you this many apples" in coffee shops and for services and for beautiful things to adorn your bodies and yet, aside from the tree, nobody ever has apples. Even the apple farmer does not actually own the bucket of apples, the land on which they were grown or the life-energy force that runs through his body that was expended to help to cultivate them.

For a time this exchange was represented on your planet by gold, or storages of gold, but the physical gold, no longer matches the amount of I.O.U. notes that are in circulation, and so it is meaningless. The exchange is now represented by the idea of exchange. It is fiction.

It is a way to tell each other: "You're good for 'it'. I know you're good for 'it'. So, give me that paper and I will give you a coffee. Next time I will give you this paper and you will give me a slice of cake. We will pass it back and forth for all eternity." That is, until you no longer need the note from your brother because you want to give them the coffee, knowing they are you.

It's a clever system in that it has, in part, worked for you, but in many parts has caused so much distraction and confusion and mixing of one's idea of worth with something that has nothing to do with them. It also has only been working for some of you and not for all.

---

1   the choice of apple as the fruit in this example and Vagrein's use of the term 'first apple' suggest a connection between the biblical story of Adam's consumption of the forbidden fruit of the Tree of Knowledge, leading humanity's exile from the Garden of Eden. Returning to a needs-based economy is being suggested as a return to times of peace and well-being.

For when you think about it, how is it possible that if you are paid 4$ for an hour of your time you are worth less than if you are paid 2000$ for an hour of your time? Both the 4 and 2000 are simply numbers written, not even on paper anymore but written electronically, in some computer somewhere.

Is your time or energy ultimately even truly yours? Where did it come from?

Separate your sense of worth from money and see how the moment you give this entire topic less focus it will resolve itself in whatever way you choose it to.

When understanding how to find a balance between giving and taking in this world there are also those who struggle with the idea of receiving money and to you we have a simple phrase you may repeat to yourself. - "If I cannot eat I cannot serve."

The inability to receive money, is a programming that has been adopted by many that are in service, specifically to put them in a position of not being able to be in service.

Every time you accept money from someone who can afford to pay you, you are then able to serve someone who cannot afford to pay you.

In the future your understanding of the symbiotic relationship between all beings and your human family will allow you to return to a form of interaction where it is a pleasure to receive as you serve.

You will understand that it was not your mind and personality structure that divided the first cell in the zygote of your form.

You will understand that your life does not belong to you and therefore there is nothing in it for which you could take ownership. At this point, you will share openly and freely with the absolute assurance that you will be shared with in the same open and free way. You will take no more than you need, and allow each spark of the universe to manifest through you in divine inspiration, always only adding benefit, and ceasing to exploit, hoard or control. The flow of giving and receiving will once again liquefy and you will naturally solve all of your illusions of inequality, scarcity and lack.

Generosity is the act of generating more wealth for all. Your tendencies for destruction are based only on fear.

We wish you a swift journey to this experience that we know is your true, natural, state.

Many spiritual teachings accurately point to the fact that you are not the body. The 'you' in this case is not the mind either and so pointing this information out to the mind can at times confuse the mind into thinking that as one is not the body, the body has no significance.

We would point you to the understanding that while it is all illusion, there is genius and mastery behind the illusion. There is no point of the illusion that is not written specifically for certain potentials to be available to an entity.

Your body is perfectly formulated to allow you to have the experiences you have chosen to have in this existence. It allows you locomotion, communication and cognitive reasoning. It allows you to create the illusion of time and location and to then navigate within it. It is a vehicle which both determines and is determined by your life story.

The body is as spiritual as any other aspect of you. In fact, it is made up first of spirit more so than matter. Matter is a concept that a limited scientific understanding has created in order to explain the un-explainable - for there is truly no satisfactory way to explain to a mind within existence how any of existence exists. The logical mind cannot digest an explanation of existence so science has come up with approximations while omitting some of the information.

On one level of understanding you are not the body but on another you completely are the body, for you are inseparable from all aspects of your existence and all aspects of all of existence.

To re-frame: You are not the body because you are not ONLY the body.

It is in the word 'only' where the balance lies. It is required as there is an imbalance in the majority of your collective towards believing that one is only the body and not spirit.

The body is only one aspect of you, we praise your physical vehicles, we are in awe of them, we see the beauty in them that you do not see. Know that they are not the full aspect of you.

NOT ONLY THE BODY

You are the body, the spirit, the intellect, the emotions, the internal and the external. You are every other-self. You are **All-That-Is**. You are not only the intellect, you are not only the emotions you are not only the body. You are the collection of all of these things. You are the experiences. You are the witness of the experience, but you are also the experience.

In the beginning, your species had to learn about what is known to be survival because it is not a usual or everyday thing to be attached to something which vibrates as slowly as matter. It takes effort to be slowed down to a speed where the senses can take over - great amounts of effort - and it is this effort, this concentration in physical form, that requires you to sleep - not the actual physical fatigue of your vessels.

A child, upon arriving in your world, arrives with the very minimum of responsibility for self that is possible. This is because infants are in the process of learning how to remain attached to their bodies. To facilitate this responsibility for the protection of the physical vehicle is temporarily deferred to the adults in the life of the child.

You cannot arrive on Earth as fully mature adults because the physical vessel would not maintain the mind-body-spirit connection long enough for the rhythms necessary to sustain what you call life to take hold. Even in the case of your very young, there are many unexplained 'deaths' where the spirit is unable or rather, unwilling to continue to make the effort of learning to remain so wholly attached. Incarnation is not the natural state of consciousness.

There are seeming needs that are required to remain attached to the physical vessel; hunger, thirst & shelter. During the first phases of evolution, humans were very much survival-oriented. What was not understood then is that these needs were never true requirements of your being. They were desires to experience the entirety of the physical vessel - agreements that you collectively made in order to set up a system of how things 'should' be. It was cooperation which put in place the beliefs that more than what was available was needed for physical life.

There are other consciousnesses on your planet which made other decisions and do not have the same requirements. An example of such is your vegetable and plant lifeforms which do not believe themselves to need anything other than what is naturally provided for them.

This is not to say that you currently do not require food, water or protection from the elements, only that this, as every other thing, is and has been, a choice.

As you progressed, survival became less of a perceived urgency. Once you started working together and forming your villages with agriculture and shared shelters, there was the opportunity to accelerate on a holistic path sooner. There were cultures who did chose this direction and arrived at great levels of self-awareness and communion with All-There-Is, but the majority of the planet chose to bring their learned habits of fear and urgency into the new and relatively calmer state of being. In choosing this they brought with them new threats. Eventually these threats were no longer beasts and the elements of the planet, but each other. The divisions that were set in place trained your people further towards division.

In the past 100 years or so the veil of this division has begun to drop. Technology has advanced so that it becomes increasingly easy for you to feel comfortable in your physicality. You have been creating permission slips for yourselves to live longer and process the world around you better. There is less fear that your diseases cannot be eradicated[1] or that the things you consume are poison. As this is happening you are also exchanging more and more information to the contrary. You talk about how disease is spreading and poisons are multiplying. Your collective consciousness is becoming stronger - pulling further towards truth rather than fear, and yet you remain in an uncertainty.

Presently there is a new physical evolution arriving in conjunction with your mental, emotional and spiritual upgrades. These upgrades are occurring all around you and your scientists, not understanding the full scope of the situation, will try to project all manner of hypothesis on it. Your bodies are being altered via natural process to allow you to arrive at a conscious absorption and integration of higher energy transmissions.

There are already beings on your planet with certain structures and codifications in the physical form that are not entirely supported by both your societal and environmental structures. These beings have the sensations of not fitting in, and physically, periods of deep fatigue. As these upgrades occur the seeming discomfort will reduce while those who are not yet codified may struggle with the new energy systems.

Humans are an interesting animal on your planet for they are not entirely native to it and some of you are less native to it than others. Those with

---

1 The fear that you are currently experiencing relating to present day ideas of sickness and virus is not paragon-able with the earlier fear, and perhaps acceptance, that you were as impotent in the face of disease as you are in the face of tectonic activity. While there still remains a collective fear of disease there is also a belief that you are, with your tools of manipulation, able to eliminate perceived bacterial and viral threat.

bodies in the process of this new evolution will feel the effects of that configuration. The ways to alleviate it are first and foremost acceptance of it as a trade-off for some of the less known or less understood benefits of the physical vessels that you are housed in.

An analogy may be a farm vehicle that is plowing land. It plows very well and was built for that. If you try to do the same work with a sports car pulling a rake it will be very inefficient. It will take far more time and be quite exhausting for the sports car. This does not mean there's anything wrong with the sports car. The car is not understanding what it is capable of and that it is certainly not meant to be plowing a field.

Presently there are so many of you who are affected by the same fatigue. It is in part because you are able to process energies that are not on a visible level and convert those energies into something that can then be transmitted to the so-called tractor. You are still expected to plow the field. This will not be for much longer. Once you get on to some nice flat asphalt you will feel much better. We assure you that you would not be here in the exact configuration that you are, if it was not necessary.

The consciousness housed in these bodies is faster and at a higher frequency than earlier versions of humans and therefore it takes even more effort to slow down to a speed where an attachment to the physical vessel is stabilized. These beings do much of their recovery in sleep or horizontal positioning. The discomfort is also in part because they have not been taught tools to speed up their bodies to match more seamlessly with their vibrational signatures.

The body is ultimately an illusion and the illusion. Solutions to an illusory problem are themselves illusions and therefore able to solve the problem on the same level it was created. Your body is very wise. To force oneself to sleep, or eat, or any other function of maintenance of the human body is a form of plugging one's ears to a divine wisdom. If you are wanting to command your body what to do, there are ways of doing so. If you are wanting to find more alignment then it is time to listen to your body.

DIET

Vagrein talks very seldom about diet and what we should or should not consume. I decided to compile and include these small bits of information with the book as they are universal enough and respect personal choices enough not to influence or manipulate anyone who's will is to act outside of these guidelines.

At any time one makes a change to their physical habits of consumption they alone are the only authority and guide. Please hold this in your awareness and listen only to yourself as you read this and any other section that holds suggestions on your health.

We are at times reluctant to give practical advice on your 3D plane as we believe in the choice of each individual to find their own path in all arguments, in all decisions and all circumstances. Everything is your choice and your beliefs about everything that you are in contact with will influence your situation with them. Therefore one could eat what is considered an unhealthy diet on your planet and as long as that one believes it was well for their body they will have no consequence from this diet. It may be hard to hold the belief that what you eat is healthy for you regardless and it is your thinking about it that creates its value for you are in the process of awakening to the ideas of what is good for and not good for your body - even if much of the information you currently digest is incorrect.

In terms of diet, our blanket statement would be to endeavor to keep it as close as possible to foods that have come directly from the planet. These foods have evolved with you in order to sustain life. All processed foods and human created foods are not optimum for you. This is especially relevant for those experiencing fatigue and any difficulty in their physical form. It is not a mystery. Everything has already been provided for you. We applaud your creativity, however. Your idea of what is desired and what is actually desired by the body are not congruent.

Make sure your diet also includes a fair amount of taking care of yourself on an emotional level. We would not restrict any foods that bring you pleasure currently. You would do well to simply increase your awareness about where your foods come from and what they're doing inside of your body. Feel how you react to what you consume, for what you consume becomes what your body is made of.

As your frequency increases you'll naturally be drawn to foods that are better for you. As your self-love increases you will naturally be drawn to foods that are better for you. You know on an instinctual and biological level which foods are good for you.

Your brain is capable of making changes to your unconscious patterns, and so optimizing your brain function will also aid in this endeavor. This includes discovering and researching foods that is help your brain to function and consuming more of those foods. Staying hydrated and practicing any activity that allows both hemispheres of your brain to work in conjunction. Change in any way and learning is much more facilitated in this manner.

There is no reason why one cannot live on nothing but plasma or on only water or only dandelions except that there are beliefs, and a collective belief, that it is not possible or it is not healthy or the body needs certain things. The mind and the body do not truly exist, what does exist is the consciousness that is writing the script.

If that consciousness writing the scripts decides to write the script where food is no longer necessary, then food is no longer necessary. The person that is writing may decide that food is no longer necessary and yet still believes food is necessary on some level and has the physical repercussions of that.

But ultimately the script reading and writing is up to you. There are very skilled writers who have written the story that food is not necessary and there are very skilled writers who have written the story that one must eat animals and there are very skilled writers who have written a story that one must eat humans[2]. What are you wanting to write? What are you wanting to read?

Anything goes.

In terms of practices and non-physical diet meditation is always suggested. The intention being the clearing of mind, for it is not so much one's action that brings results, but their intention.

We also encourage finding what pleases you in terms of joy, what makes you laugh, what makes you smile and doing more of those things, leaning in the direction of your natural excitement and fun, and taking the time to ask and check in with yourself: "What do I need in this moment?" Then meet that need even if it goes against the advice we have just given you and even if it goes against the advice of what you've heard from many others.

---

2   *This last part of the statement was included to: 1) Make the point that we have, at all times, , choice on all topics. 2) Reinforce the position of neither condemnation or endorsement of any of our choices, and 3) remind the reader that there are currently practices occurring on our planet that we hold a preference of ignoring. When one is in a state of ignorance or denial they renege their ability to make a choice on the topic.*

The body is your ally. Your body, no matter the circumstance, can never be a limitation to what you can share or the light you can spread in the world. You do not need your body to spread your light. You are light.

Your body, when not in perfect functioning order according to your imposed criteria is not something external making it inconvenient for you to do the things that you would rather be doing. It is you talking to yourself via the tools which that aspect of yourself has to get your attention. What is wanted here is a healing of this relationship.

The body cares for you unconditionally. It is always in service to you. Every perceived misalignment or pain or discomfort is your body loving you unconditionally. It is its way of communicating with you. What is perhaps not the case is you understanding or listening to the communication from your body. One way to understand more fully what your body is trying to tell you, on top of letting go of this conditionality - which only makes the ailment louder- would be to dive directly into the feeling of the discomfort and ask 'What are you trying to tell me?'. This bypasses the mind because your awareness is not on trying to find the answer but trying to hear the answer. Try it now.

The body is a skilled poet and each being is completely unique. We would suggest that beginning to love your body as much as it loves you would be of the utmost value. Once you take this beautiful aspect of yourself on as a collaborator as opposed to a character who is trying to spoil the fun, you will be able to hear the suggestions that it is making to you.

Your bodies are absolutely miraculous and working with you at all times. Many symptoms that you have are pointing you towards a alteration of action in circumstance and not the resolution of the symptoms.

If one has a cold and decides not to go to a party to stay home to rest, it may not be because they need to stay home and rest. It may be because there was something or someone at that party that their higher self knew was not in their best interest to engage with in that moment in time. You have to understand that your

YOUR BODY : YOUR BEST ALLY

body and the wisdom of your body is not just about your body as the body is working at all times in conjunction with your whole self. Your higher self will use any means to lead you and guide you to what is best for you and will use the body to do so.

**W**e remind you that all is occurring in the present and that time does not truly exist so one can release any ailment in any now, if that is their choice. It is common however that people choose to experience pain, discomfort, disease or ailment in the body to have the opportunity to have the experience of letting go of these.

There is still a propensity towards focusing upon the body as if it were some sort of hindrance to one's path. We would love to remind you that a blockage or trauma stored in your body, no matter the discomfort level, no matter the distraction level, is in service to you. The issue exists for you have not yet learned some lesson. We would also like to remind you that while you would like to clear trauma or blockages, everything is always and always will be in it's own time and with it's own pace and any sort of insistence is a form of believing that one knows better than What-Is.

One does not.

This arrogance is a form of procrastination from focusing on what is a more true subject of focus for a being at any given point of time. When one is focused on what is not working, they are not focusing on what is working. When one focuses on what is working, one cannot focus on what is not. This is the secret to your blocks.

Your emotional and mental and physical bodies are intricately linked. The body is not directly affected by trauma. It is like a tape recorder in that it is waiting for you to hit the playback button so that you can have the conversation with yourself about what happened and what you felt about it. When traumatic experiences get stored in the body it is to allow you to have a break from what is not possible to process at the time emotionally and records the information for a later time. Then you still have the opportunity to learn what you chose to learn by having that experience in the first place. The body has the wisdom within it to tell you how to let it go. If you are to go and talk to your body parts or your pain points within your body you will find very quickly that they have their own voices. These voices are often your own voice from a seeming earlier point in time.

BLOCKS + TRAUMA IN THE BODY

To release this trauma one may focus on the body to find the point that seems to hold some form of seeming negative experience. Focus on the part of the body that has this registration[1] for you and hit the play button by asking it "What do you have to tell me?" It will often begin to tell you the story of what you believe happened to you and what you could do to resolve it within yourself; in forgiveness, learning and love.

Physical pain can be seen as a sensation to relax into. It is a focusing. You may use your physical pain to focus into relaxation. Every time you feel pain you can use that as a bell to say relax and every part of your body that is able to relax, in that moment you can relax, even if there is a part that is contracted.

We wish you could all put on your human suits like Halloween costumes and take it off as easily. It would be absolutely delightful if you were to understand that your bodies are these very intelligent systems, but they are systems within which you are navigating. You are wearing these systems. These systems have sensors that feel out the environment with which you are in and send information back to you. However there is a confusion. Everyone believes that they are the system.

These are your vehicles. If you scrape up against the curb with your car there will be a scratch on your front bumper and if you ten years later look at your front bumper there will still be the scratch but all it is saying is don't scrape up against the curb. Then when you go to the mechanic and you have it painted and repaired and it's good as new and you have learned not to drive so close to the curb. The blocks, traumas, contractions and scars are nothing more than a reminder of how far you have come, and that it's time to have a tune up.

---

1   *From the Latin 'regesta': to list*

T he word 'healing' in itself has the connotations that something is not as it should be, and would be better if it were changed.

To understand any one sentence in the story of one's life one would need to zoom to a level of awareness of all the fractals and all the potentials that could come from each sentence, word, letter and drop of ink.

When a combination of circumstances seems to point to a pattern in the life of an entity there is the natural tendency to judge the pattern as positive or negative. As humans you tend not to see positive patterns, only what you believe to be negative and this judging is actually what is causing the pain on a far deeper level than the physical pain could possibly ever cause. The judgment is what allows you to hold on to the pain. The judgment is what allows you to fear the pain, to remember it, and to recreate it for yourself.

Physical traumas and disturbances in the field of an entity are there for a reason but the reason is not for punishments or being out of alignment or for having had the 'wrong' thoughts. This, as every other catalyst is, a beautiful opportunity to learn what it is you came here wanting to learn.

Most chronic or longer lived physical ailment is of this nature. It is a persistent, ambitious, and very loving soul communicating that it's so much desires in this lifetime to learn a particular lesson.

This is why healing never truly occurs and never truly can occur. There is nothing unwell, unhealed or imperfect about your body no matter what level of health or wellness you are believe you are experiencing. The body is always doing exactly what it is meant to be doing. It is at times asking you to pay more attention to it in regards to what you believe to be important in your life. At times it is attempting to heal a relationship with you that is long overdue for what is known as healing.

A beneficial tool for what you think of as healing: Feel into and understand the reasons why whatever discomfort, pain, illness, disease or disability that currently appears in your experience is serving you. There will be reasons why what you are believing

IT IS IMPOSSIBLE TO HEAL

you want to be healed is serving you or other-selves in a benevolent way. There is nothing that can-be without the approval of the All-That-Is and therefore seeking this answer or even simply asking this question will automatically pull you into closer alignment with Source's perspective on the topic. If you like, imagine that the being wanting to be healed is not you but someone else. Then imagine all the potential and possible reasons why not only a physical level, but on a holistic and complete human level, the discomfort may be benefiting. From there, you will have insight, as to the possible reasons why this is your present reality.

You may even discover that you are quite pleased to have your reality.

All the beings you have met on your 'healing journey' you would not know. All the compassion you have mastered through your own suffering you would not know. You would not be able to read this passage if there was not this ailment. You would not be able to seek out remedies or methods of healing.

There are many of you who have come to have physical ailments in order to create the new medical system. Without problems on the level of which you perceive problems, there would not be those who are here to seek solutions. Those have written in the stars a contract with the collective to create the mutually beneficial outcome of all of your life stories. You are choosing this honour over your personal comfort. If you can override and accept your condition fully you may remain in the middle ground.

The path that you will be led down, or are being led down, because of this supposed inconvenient ailment, is different from the path that you would be heading down, if you did not have this ailment. If you are able to find the reasons that help you to understand why it is perfect for your exact experience to be what it is then you can move out of victim-hood and into ownership with appreciation for your current state of being.

Where healing is then perceived what has actually has occurred is acceptance, love and the reorganization of situation and circumstance to a situation and circumstance which is now benefiting the being more than the previous situation and circumstance. In that new reality the ailment is no longer the most expansive path for the being. Something has changed directionally and the timeline that held the disease is no longer required.

Before the "healing" the ailment was the most beneficial for that being at that time. Even if the perception of the world claims that there is an optimum version of a human being there is no one optimum version of the body. The only optimum version of the body is the exact version of each body in this time and space, otherwise it could not exist.

You are already healed and yet you do not like this healed version of you. You have a preference for another version. The true healing comes when the desire for something different than What-Is no longer produces discomfort within you.

This is not to say that you cannot or should not seek a version of you that would be more conducive to what you want to do in your life, but this will happen naturally. In fact, the kaleidoscope of circumstance that arrives from the seeking of relief or soothing or healing are often the reason an ailment is in place.

For example: If part of your blueprint and exploration for being here includes the act of being healed outside of your conventional medical systems, then you will need to have some form of ailments to heal to be able to do that exploration.

Healing, in the way that you collectively have it defined, is a natural phenomenon as each being begins to listen more wholly to their body, and each being begins to accept wholly the What-Is, and each being sees the beauty in the vessel that they are housed in.

There are of course on practical levels, many things that many can and will tell you and teach you on how to heal. Many of them will be valid for you as you will be able to use those permission slips in conjunction with the growth that you are currently under to find the solution that is most beneficial to you.

When beings awaken to the fact that they are capable of healing without external sources, there will be far less distortion in the field. There is a potential of a future reality where it is no longer necessary to take the advice of an other-self on what is one's only and most precious physical gift.

This is not to say that in the moments where you have the belief that allopathic medicine is required for relief that you should not partake in it. Indeed it is possible that the ailment exists specifically for you to have the desire to visit conventional doctors or take their advice which of course would lead you down a timeline and story-line that is entirely perfect in that it is where you are.

There is the option to work around the problem by no longer seeing it as a problem and reintegrating it with your full being; seeing it as no different from pleasure - we are referring to pain - and integrate it in that fashion. However, that route is only relevant to whom it is relevant.

To many, many others there is another story-line awaiting in the pot of ink.

Our suggestion to all those who have physical ailments would be to focus on accepting All-That-Is, as equal, benevolent and pure love this includes the pain, the treatment, the emotions one has about this subject and all circumstances that circle around it. Define the sensation as simply 'What-Is' without any form of explanation or self-judgment. Reach for total acceptance and surrender.

Take rest when needed. Follow the inspirations that your body affords you for nourishment, touch and water. Listen.

The breath is what connects the body to the non-physical realm. It is what keeps the body animated with consciousness. It is not studied by your scientists at this time in this way though it has been deeply studied by your mystics. There are ways and means of breathing to achieve specific results if so desired - Intention is always the captain of any ship, and breathing with intention means that you can navigate to new land. If you so choose.

You have access to body and bodies that are not housed within your physical body. Your physical body is only the end result of a collection of energy that becomes, according to your perception tools - the senses - visual, auditory, taste, olfactory and tactile. Your actual comprehensive body is far larger than your physical body, and there are tools that these bodies have that you as you, not as your physical body but as you, have access to right Now.

When you refer to intuition, you have a sense that this is not in your sensory body. This is correct. There is a space - not in the sense of location - that seems to be 'somewhere'. You are able to perceive intuition as having a location even though it does not have one in what you understand as the reality of location. If you become accustomed to locating this non-local 'somewhere', you will be able to listen to this font more clearly and without having to search for it, as you already know where it is. This is the skill required for accessing higher consciousness. Accessing this non-location 'space' is the skill that our author uses when she tunes into us. She has found our 'location'. It is as simple as that and we meet her there.

We can use an example that is often used and we are sure you have heard in the past but it does take turning to complete mush for a caterpillar to become a butterfly. It is used so often that it is completely overlooked that it is true. If you were to open the cocoon mid metamorphosis not only would this un-embodied caterpillar no longer have the possibility of becoming a butterfly as the goo would seep out onto the forest floor but you would discover that there is absolutely nothing in there.

On a level

The Non-Physical Physical Body

of sensation it is very painful for the caterpillar but there's inner wisdom to not open the cocoon during this period. The caterpillar, as much pain as it feels, does not bite through the cocoon and try to escape for it would mean certain death. We're using this metaphor perhaps to explain that while you have sensations now in this time of change, it is not necessary to open the cocoon and poke around in the goo.

As one undertakes a conscious awareness of the spiritual aspects of their life they also undertake an awareness of other, though not separate, non-physical aspects of existence: energies, collective vibrations, and all form of extra and ultra-sensory contribution to experience. As all humans are capable of allowing heightened extrasensory perception, when coming to know the energy that animates their own lives they will have access or contact with the residue of all other energies, to a greater or lesser degree. One side effect of having these subtle channels open is confusion. However, confusion only arises when one is attempting to give meaning to new situations based upon old understandings. When one notices new forms of energy, new feelings, sensations, experiences running through their system and tries to identify these based upon their understandings of existence from a 3D perspective, inaccurate labels will get applied to the sensations.

A sensation of a higher energy running through a physical vessel is unlike typical human emotions and sensations and, if placed in comparison with them, could be labeled as more intense. If you were to take this labeling further and try to identify the sensation and emotion connected with these energies, your vocabulary, depending upon your current state of perspective, may settle upon a term or label that you are already familiar with: Anxiety, fear, sorrow, or on the other end of the spectrum: delight, excitement, mania, ecstasy. All of these labels and terms are incorrect and detrimental to the experiencing of the energy unfolding in you. Labeling in this way will delay the integration of the new energies. It will slow the progress of the physical vessel and the mental and emotional bodies from accepting and preparing themselves for higher and more subtle versions of the same new energies. What is actually being felt cannot be labeled in terms that the mind currently holds and, even searching for a new label with other new vocabulary would be futile for the energies to which we are referring, do not exist on a level where vocabulary as you use it, is commonplace. If one entity, or being, or individuation wants to express these levels of energies to another being, or entity or individuation, they simply transmit the sensation of it and no label is needed.

What we see happen, when new energies are allowed into a system and are being labeled, is that the Being that has accepted these energies, can find themselves struggling in a period of adjustment where their mind is trying to apply an understanding to the changes and what is happening to them, and we say to you that this struggling is unnecessary.

To alleviate this struggle, we suggest an immersion, or diving into of the energy itself and if the mind needs an occupation during this bath, it may take the role of a curious spectator while you, as awareness, soak in the new sensations of energy. As you soak in them without needing to categorize or explain, simply staying to observe and be with the sensation, you'll find that it becomes far easier to integrate and accept these frequencies and with your permission, acceleration will continue on its trajectory; taking along with it, your growth.

It is clear that to perform such a task, silence and isolation are beneficial. You may meditate. However do not underestimate the possibility of it occurring during any task at all; while in the company of other-selves, or while during one's more imperative daily tasks. For in truth all that would be needed would be intention. One could ask their higher self with intention to gently and without labeling, integrate these energies and adopt them as one's own. If you can embody the energies of change with the curiosity of a child, with that innocence and non judgment of self and circumstance then any change is smoother, more enjoyable and will come to its most fruitful end.

We would also like to add that you are always in change. You just don't know that you are. And if every moment could be seen with that same energy of newness then the same feeling and results would occur.

ACTIVITY : SENSING BEYOND THE BODY

Here I will add a short visualization that came through right before one of Vagrein's sessions that ties in with this topic:

Get settled and see if you can sense the energy beyond your senses. So, use the ears beyond your ears and as your eyes are open sense into the vision beyond the physically seeing eyes. Try to see if you can tap into that natural vibration that is always present...

The Italian word 'sottofondo' describes this nicely. It is the background or an undercurrent, as it's literal translation would be 'the below-background'.

Tune into this below-background vibration of all of existence. For me it's very palpable when I stop and tune into it. Maybe by pausing your reading now, after this chapter you can sense it as well with those extra senses that we all have.

Before continuing, try to become aware of a part of your body that has always been there, but you haven't really paid much attention to it. Maybe your smallest toe on your left foot. Sense into it. Feel it. You can see how it's very present and always been there, but you don't normally put your attention on it.

Well these other senses, are the same. They are just there, and they are part of your greater body, and you can just move your awareness, outside of your physical skin, your skin line, and you have access to all this other richness and ability to just know.

Before reading on, take a moment to quiet your mind and tune these muscles now.

The body is not a singular thing but a community of cells. The cells each have their function of reproducing, repairing, cooperating and dying so that you can function in your body in the physical world. The physical world is also made up of the community of cells. To allow cells to last longer or allow them to function longer one must undertake the process of changing beliefs that do not support this desire.

Both you as your mind and your cells currently believe they have an expiry date or a time which reproduction will no longer be possible. Interestingly humans as a collective have adopted this thought also in regard to your civilization and are heading towards a time when you too believe that reproduction in the form of children will no longer be possible. Reproduction is infinitely possible. On a cellular level this means cells splitting without the polarity of male and female; just naturally splitting to reproduce themselves in a process of cloning. Since you cannot take your cells and poke at them directly, put them in classrooms and teach them they are immortal you can teach yourself the lesson instead. For what is learned on the macro is learned in the micro. If you were to understand that you truly are immortal, that everything about you is immortal, then your cells will begin to naturally understand this as well.

Your thoughts control reality also on the level of what you call scientific reality. Science will slowly or quickly, depending upon you, announce their discoveries in this direction. These discoveries will be permission slips for you to live much longer than you do currently, much more well than you do currently, and with much more energy than you do currently.

There's no need for the body to fail and die. Being concerned with the aging process at all speaks to a remaining fear of death. For if one was not afraid of death, why would it be necessary to maintain their longevity? The natural process of trees shedding their leaves is not mourned by the tree and if your cells are ceasing to reproduce it may be because there is something more interesting to come when that process is through.

You still have this fear of death, be-cause you still have not wo-

DEATH + AGING OF THE PHYSICAL BODY

ken up to the realization that you were never 'alive' in the first place. It is, however, in part noble that you have chosen to become attached to your own unique experience here. This points to remembering the desire with which you came into incarnation in the first place.

There is the possibility of worrying less about remaining alive. This will in no way affect the actual amount of so-called time that you are alive. In fact, worrying about the transition phase is a great way to accelerate it's arrival, due to the law of attraction.

Those who renounce the body completely do not do so not out of courage, they do so out of fear. This fear states that it is only by renouncing the body completely that one can avoid death. It amounts to intellectualism making the claim: I am not the body and therefore I will exist eternally.

It is true that you will exist eternally, for you already do exist eternally, but this is not conditional on a renunciation of the body. Once one integrates the fact that one is in this illusion, or reality - which are interchangeable in this case - and sharing one's existence with the body they do have to face that at some point that relationship will end.

On an intellectual level, renouncing the body seems to be the only way to cheat death. However, in this renunciation one simultaneously rejects, renounces and cheats life.

The only way to avoid the death process is to be truly alive in every moment. It is not enough to wake and wander through existence for your days. Those who are truly alive have the spark of the Creator in them and are fulfilling each of their own individual prophecies. This, of course, is optional too. There is no consequence to not following your spark. The only consequence of any action imaginable is expansion.

While the body has the illusion of ceasing to exist, it is not even the body that has ceased to exist upon death. It is only the image created through your spiritual decision to create a body that ceases to exist. All this occurs within the equally illusory image created through your spiritual decision to create a world in which one could be alive in the first place.

The concept of death is an assumption. There has never been nor ever will be anyone who dies, for from the perspective of each individual, death is only something that they have experienced, up until their own presumable death, as an observer on an external level. So throughout beings lives they witness, people and animals and vegetation around them die, or what they claim to be as dying. With this experience they have drawn the conclusion that they too will die one day. However no one has ever died from a first person perspective. Death is no more significant to your soul than passing a bowel-movement is.

It is as equally probable that you will never die as it is that you will. In one hundred years time you may still be alive and they may invent a medicine that you take every morning that increases your longevity and this will be your permission slip to continue to believe that you can live forever. On this level one must remember that death is a concept within the illusion of this particular construction of what is called reality, however there is no proof that anyone dies. What does happen when one seems to die is that a decision to move in a specific direction in the never-ending story-line requires an occurrence of what you have labeled as death to continue along with the next simultaneous chapter.

What is happening when a loved one seems to have died, is that the image on a screen of a being that you interacted with no longer interacting with you. That is not proof that they have vanished from existence or what you call, died - with all your labels and assumptions of what that means. It is not proof that they do not exist. That is not proof that their essence does not continue. It is only proof that their body no longer moves - If that is even proof.

The essence of the portion of consciousness that you know as a loved one does not change or leave in any way whatsoever. What changes or leaves is your perception of it. You perceive of a relative or being as being alive and then you perceive of them as being dead. This in part is because your culture and the way the system has been set up for you has allowed you to believe this and it serves you, so we would not say that it is necessary to not believe it, but on the more expanded level your loved one was never alive and so he did not die.

When a relationship that brought value to your experience seems to have come to an end it can create emotions within you based upon the beliefs on that subject. This is natural because of your conditioning on this subject but we would suggest that you remember that these emotions come up because there is something about your beliefs on the subject that is not in line with the universal truths.

If you are sad that you will never be able to speak to them again then you are hinting, through your emotions, that you can speak to them again, perhaps simply in another fashion. If while sensing into that thought the feeling shifts to a more positive nature then it is the one that is more true. How can you speak to them again? Well that is up to you, but we guarantee you that you can. The simple action of remembering one who has past connects the living with that energy form with that consciousness and therefore there is more access to that consciousness. In this tapestry you are connected with this being whether or not they have a physical form.

Every-time one who has passed comes into your mind in memory there is part of you that knows that this is not just a thought, it is not just a memory, there is that sensation of the essence of this being joining you in your time space reality, joining you in your thought-form, in your memories, in your feeling state.

Holding a conditioning as to what it means to be alive and what it means to be dead causes you to forget and instead of basking in the essence of the being in the moments that they are with you, you immediately go to the sense of loss of this being because they are no longer in physical form. If you were able to allow yourself for a brief moment to forget that you miss them and instead focus on being with them you will notice with practice that they are very much more with you now than they ever could have been in physical form. You, in your own time and space, will even be able to call to them with your mind and they will respond to you in their voice, and they will respond to you with their essence, for they are part of consciousness in exactly the same way that you are.

This does not mean we are talking about ghosts who are stuck some place in some plane of limbo. Many have created a story to explain this possibility of being able to speak with those who have passed. It does not mean that they are suffering. What it means is that they have returned to the global consciousness in the way and the means that we are and that the essence of you is right now. If you meet them with your essence and for the moment put down the idea that you must meet them with your physical form you have immediate access to all of those who have been here before. All reality is simultaneous and all is Now.

We guarantee to you that it is possible to be immortal - and that you all are.

Death is one of those subjects that is so very confused in your world and so very misunderstood and makes you all feel terrible because you are all so confused about it. Every time you have a close being that passes you are in a position where you are being offered the opportunity to no longer feel as confused about this subject and no longer have to feel negative aspects of it and so are able to become more free.

On another level there is also the beautiful truth that for every being that passes, their soul gets added back to the infinite intelligence and they then become, possibly more so, available to all those whom they loved in their lives as guides, or messengers.

We would love for you to know what a celebration transition is. It is a choice it is on the part of the one that has transitioned. Often, a transition happens because the one who is transitioning knows that it is the perfect moment for all those around them to push the boundaries of their current belief systems.

There is only love. And so much more so when all the bags have been put down and forgotten. You must simply remember that you are far more powerful than you believe yourself to be.

Just beyond your physical body is all that with which you identify as you that is non-physical: Your thoughts and emotions. What is known as 'mind' is a collaboration between these thoughts and emotions - both sourced from what seems to be external stimuli - then filtered through the vibrational frequency of your being based upon its current desire for expansion. For this reason we have grouped together in this chapter your emotional and intellectual life in 'the thinking-feeling mind'.

Neither your thoughts nor your feelings are personal to you as an individuation. In the same way your body is on loan from the earth your mind is on loan from the **ether**. Any identification with your thoughts and emotions is an unnecessary misunderstanding which brings only confusion and suffering. You as an eternal being are experiencing your thoughts and emotions in the same way you experience shifting clouds or a sunny sky.

Thoughts can create emotion and emotion can create thoughts, but you -as what you truly are- cannot create either. You are the filter through which both pass.

The mind is a tool. The thinking aspects of the mind exist in order to allow for communication and structuring of action while the emotional side allows for a gauging of how aligned action and thought is with true intention and source energy. Emotions signal the validity or non validity of your thoughts with Knowing. Knowing is the truth of existence. Intelligence is the realization of the already present connection between the brain and the heart.

It is never a case of integrating the heart with the brain or the brain with the heart as the term 'integration' implies separation, and this is not so. Your heart can already encompass the energetic field that you attribute to your brain, but the brain as a physical organ does not allow an encompassing energetically of the heart for it speaks a different language. The only way the brain can allow space for the heart energy is by moving out of the way. It is simple mechanics.

To have All-That-Is be All-That-Is, all is necessary. Let us first unpack thoughts: You find yourself

THE THINKING FEELING MIND

in a version of the All where the manifestation that you call thoughts exist floating around willy-nilly in all of consciousness. Perceiving yourselves as separate beings, each one of you can receive these packets, or flashes, which turn into thought, based upon your receptivity to them.

Who created thoughts or whose are they? They are no-one's. They are the One's and in reality there is only one thought, but what you perceive as a never ending stream of consciousness is not yours in the way you identify with it. It is no one's. To explain this further, you may use the example of the wind:

The wind does not belong to anyone. It just Is. Sometimes it blows in your face, and moves your hair and gives you a chill and passes through you. Thoughts are similar and yet, as with the wind, you do not have control aside from where you position yourself in an environment as to whether or not you will be chilled by the wind.

With thoughts, you may also position yourself to either be blown by the thoughts or not. You may shelter yourself from thoughts that you do not prefer by positioning yourself out of their range vibrationally. It is only when one identifies only with their thoughts that they stand in a hurricane and allow themselves to be blown over. If you did not identify with your thoughts you would simply move out of the way in the same way as when there's a heavy wind you do not say 'This is where I meant to stand. This is my position.'

The more of you who learn to move out of the way, the less hurricane thoughts will be added to the collective and eventually, there will be no storms.

Yes, you are part of a field of infinite potential. The only mechanism that allows your existence is this field of infinite potential. It allows all things, every iteration, simultaneously. Because of this field all thoughts exist simultaneously and all thoughts belong to all of the field. This field allows for any entity to pluck from it any thought at any time. None of these thoughts belong to that entity specifically, as they are part of the field and therefore belong to the entirety of it and any entities that would pluck that thought from it. So your thoughts are not your own, they are one of any number of infinite thoughts in the infinite field of potentials.

You can know if the thoughts you are choosing are in alignment with your true inner desires for learning by paying attention to the emotions generated by a chosen thought. If they are positive you are approaching an aligned version of who you would like to be. If the emotions are uncomfortable you are distancing yourself from the version of who you want to be in order to have the opportunity of knowing more of yourself.

We have spoken of your ability to choose at any time whatever reality you want to be experiencing. The majority of your species habitually choose the same thoughts from the field and choose to identify with these thoughts because they continue to believe that they **are** their thoughts.

You are not your mind. You are not your emotions. Your thoughts are not yours. And while they influence your experience and perhaps seem outside of your direct control at times, they are not. You choose every thought that you have. The only question is 'Why?'. If you decide first on the 'Why?' then you will continue to choose only thoughts in line with that 'Why?'. What is yours is the choice, not the thought, not the emotion.

You now know that you are choosing with your vibration and with your frequency. At times you are deliberately choosing specific thoughts that are coming from the field. We suggest increasing the frequency with which you practice deliberate choosing. It becomes simple to allow thoughts to come and go when you do not identify with them as yours. We repeat that thoughts are not yours, only the choices are. If you choose universal love with your heart you will then choose only thoughts that align with that and no integration will be necessary.

To detach yourself from identifications with thoughts remember that you have, at your disposition, tools that are most-holy.

One tool is your mind itself and so our suggestion would be to use the mind to watch the mind to see what choices of thoughts are arising for you. This does not mean to stop thinking. What it means is to think even harder on some levels. You can do this in meditation or contemplation.

The difference would be that in meditation you may be sitting in a specific posture with your eyes closed and in contemplation you may be staring off into the sunset and actively thinking. As soon as you see that your mind has run off in this tangle-web of thoughts and rationale and stories use your mind to watch those thoughts and stories and hullabaloo that is coming through it. This could be very entertaining as well because it could be like watching some story pass before you. If you watch from a distance sooner or later compassion or a realisation of humour will dawn on you and you will see these thoughts as the innocent things that they are - simply mani-festations of thought-matter within an experience. They will most-likely slow, but it won't concern you if they do or if they don't, because you won't be identified with them, you will be identified with the non-mind that is observing the thoughts. When you are aware you are having thoughts you are already in this mind. There is no need to stop the thoughts, there is only the possibility, if you choose, to focus upon focusing upon them.

This is similar to what is called '**awareness watching awareness**' however the moment one says 'awareness watching awareness' it seems to have some sort of magical, or inaccessible or non-sustainable quality to it, and yet it is the most simple thing. It is just taking one step back from what is happening. In this way you are using your magnificent mind to enjoy and appreciate and have compassion for your magnificent mind. As awareness has no mind, from a limited perspective one cannot arrive at observing awareness if one is using the mind. The transcendence into awareness is organic and is achieved without any achievement having occurred at is it already the natural state.

Another possibility would be a more physical solution. In this case, when having many thoughts that are making one feel uncomfortable, one could go into meditation and continue to bring oneself back to the body. This is often done through an awareness of the breath - and that is why that practice is so very popular, because it is **somatically** going to take you out of your head and into your center. Some do not have success with an awareness of the breath so for them it would make more sense to have an awareness of the gut or an awareness of the heart or an awareness of the solar plexus but the main condition is to bring awareness into the body and use any sensation of the body to focus awareness away from the mind and into the physical sensations of what is. When one is focused on what is, and that can be the sensation of an ant crawling up your arm or the grass beneath your feet or whatever other sensation you are presently experiencing, positive or negative, you will eventually let go of all of the thoughts. Again, this is not 'thinking of nothing' this is focusing on something.

It is almost impossible, but not impossible with your habits of cognizance, to think of nothing so the easiest step is to think completely of only one thing. This does not stop thoughts, it just makes all thoughts more aligned with silence, which is oneness, which is the absence of thought, if that is the goal.

Remember too, that there is no need to not think. If the thoughts are not identified with then they cannot affect or harm you in any way by allowing them to be there in your mind. Continue to use your mind to reinforce the synaptic connections that 'Everything is exactly as it should be', repeat this to yourself as often as you recall to repeat it.

However, when you find you have thoughts that are running in a direction, that is no longer serving (and you will know this based upon the negative emotions that occur around the thoughts) - you may interject with your language. You may use your mind to stop and calm thoughts. You may talk with yourself. You may verbalize within your mind the words:

"These thoughts are not serving me. It is okay for them to be there. I have a preference to think about these other thoughts." At this point you may deliberately change your focus from the repetitive non-serving thoughts which provoke the negative emotional sensations within you to another topic or more deliberate choosing of thoughts on the same topic.

If you are judging yourself for having the unwanted thoughts in the first place you are still identifying with them as yours. You are identifying with them as your fault or your responsibility. Dis-identify. Judgment is never serving, except in the understanding that judgment no longer serves.

If you are distracted by your thoughts it is because you are choosing to be distracted by them. This is a sign that there is something that you do not want to face in your current experience at this moment. This is a service to you if the thing that you do not want to face is not what is meant for you at that moment.

So any form of judgment is unnecessary for any form of energy or situation or circumstance that passes through your experience. Choose to adopt a non-judgmental new practice of interrupting the thoughts, perhaps even laughing at the innocence of them and moving on to the next thing that you choose to think of instead. Any new thought that brings with it an even slight increase or relief towards positive emotion and therefore vibration is benefiting you.

If however, you have a perception that the thing you should be thinking about is more important or significant or worthy than the thing you are thinking about, it is again a question of releasing judgment of self and what one believes is the correct path for self.

NEGATIVE EMOTIONS

When your thoughts create what you would call 'negative emotion', the emotion is simply there to tell you that those thoughts are no longer relevant for you. As you think thoughts that create negative emotion within you, you will be able to release those thoughts as soon as the negative emotion gets to such a level that you have a complete understanding, that those thoughts do not serve you. Thinking in that direction and therefore feeling the negative emotion, to an extent to which you decide that it's no longer serving you, is serving you in that manner.

There is no need to fear a road that will take you towards what you call negative emotions, for there are no negative emotions. In reality all emotions are pointing you towards what works for you and what does not work for you. Therefore to a knowing of yourself more completely. Down the road you will not act outside of integrity for you will have learned more of who you are and what is integrity for you. Even if you have had negative emotions which have led you to actions that have then led to consequences or perceived consequences or which are not in alignment with who you would like to be, you will be led you to learn who you actually are. You are who you are. This game is not becoming who you would like to be. It is becoming more of who you are.

These things may not align. Your idea of who you are and who you actually are, often do not correspond. In them not being in correspondence one has the potential of causing self judgment, doubt, fear, consequences that are out of alignment with self for they are not being true to self. It is only possible to be true to self when one knows who oneself is. Life is the game of learning who one is.

Your responsibility lies with understanding more completely who you are. If this involves having thought patterns which lead you to emotions, which then either allow you to release them or to take action that is not completely in alignment with who you think you would like to be, but is more in alignment with who you are, then you will always be in a state of growth. Which you are anyway.

Feelings are a part of What-Is and they are very present in the moment they arise, sometimes overwhelmingly so. The fastest way to change a feeling state is to change the way you think as feelings are the direct barometer to whether or not one's thinking is in alignment.

When there are feelings that are persistent or recurrent and dropping the story has the feeling remain you may have attached a sense of identity to the sentiments that are more frequent in your expression. You may say to yourself or others "I am an emotional person. I have suffered from depression in the past.".

These identified-with emotional patterns could be fear, joyousness, anger, or any of the emotional expressions that you may have, however, an expression of sentiments, a feeling or an emotional state, is never true to you as identity.

Any emotional states that you frequently and habitually access that feel familiar to you are good indicators of where you have allowed unconscious programming of your mind. When noticed these programs can be transcended and let go of. Your emotional landscape does not need to be a prison sentence. It does not need to be who you are as it is not. If you are habitually not vibrating at a high frequency emotionally and it does not seem to be connected to the thoughts you are thinking now is the time to deprogram these old habits.

As we are aware of the semblance of difficulty in doing this work we would like to give you a sense of soothing that these markers, or habitual states were your choice in the first place. And that is not a judgment. It is not a criticism. It is a reminder that even the most painful sentiments and even in the most painful situations you had the nobility to choose to walk bravely into in order to learn the lessons that only those situations and those and those states of being could teach you.

No one said being human was going to be easy, and yet here you are surviving every day. We applaud you.

What are your feelings but a system of beeps and lights on a control panel? What more are they than the brake-light on your dashboard lighting up? It does not indicate that the brake light is broken - it indicates that you should probably get your brakes checked. In the case of the emotions being habitual, it is indeed your brake light firing when there is nothing wrong with the brakes and a gentle rewiring may be called for.

Do not cover up the light flashing-out its warning and think it solves the problem. Do not correct the behavior of the external persons who trigger you. This would be the equivalent of trying to turn all the traffic lights green so that you do not have to ever worry about using your breaks. You may succeed but there can always be a deer in the middle of the road.

With habitual feeling states, we prescribe habitual counter-active feeling exercises. One can begin to deliberately work oneself up into a state of feeling good without cause, many times a day until that becomes a new habit.

Remember, you also feel bad without cause. It is never the fault of the circumstance that triggers your negative feeling states, it is always an indication that you are not in alignment with your own higher self's perspective on that topic.

Interestingly, those of you who have come in with the highest desires and love for this human experience will often be those who have the experience of suffering the most because until you can understand this mechanism, the things that you see and experience in your incarnation will be perceived as so far outside of your true intentions in your higher form and the difference between this perception and the reality of who you are will be felt at a very deep level. These are those whom you call sensitive. They are indeed sensitive to anything that is out of alignment with the highest truth. The cure, however, is not to toughen up or ignore the triggers and emotions. It is instead to align oneself over and over with that higher calling of beauty, love, compassion and grace until the pain becomes a sweet reminder of all the beauty that one knows this world is capable of arriving at, thereby being a beacon for all others to aim towards that light.

Nursing Emotional Wounds

Nurse your emotional wounds until they become your points of strength and service.

We can explain this further by using your physical vessel as an example and physical sensation as a parallel to emotional feelings.

When one injures themselves physically their body sends a signal to their brain to say that they are injured. This is pain and it is useful for you to have this signal because should you not you would continue the action that led to the injury and potentially damage or lose a part of your physical being permanently or allow some process to continue to happen that would later lead to your physical end.

You understand this concept because it is very direct. Most humans do not ignore physical pain. They address it or attempt to, even if at times the cause is not understood.

Emotional pain or discomfort is the same thing. Your first step is to remove the damaging action or situation. This would be - dropping the thinking about the pain. The second step would be to look at the emotional wound and understand what needs to be done with it. If you would pretend a physical wound was not there and say to yourself "I will simply take some drugs to numb this pain and yet I will not look at it and I will not think about it." then you have the potential of infection and spreading of the problematic area. Ignoring or masking emotional pain would have similar consequences. At times the wound would heal on its own but there is always the risk of pejoration if the issue is not addressed. One must clean the wound. One must then dress and protect a physical wound.

It is the same with emotional wounding. The easiest way to do this is with self-love. To clean an emotional wound, especially one that you have been carrying around for a very long time, you may look at the beliefs that are lying beneath it and remove those beliefs. This would be like removing dirt from a scrape. Changing those beliefs to ones that better suit you, and are more in service is like putting medicine upon it - Staying with the emotion and wound, accepting it and understanding that it is healing is the dressing and protecting of the emotional wound.

You can check on it and change the bandages periodically, but were you to run away from having this wound, when it is present in your experience, you would run the risk of making it worse.

Your emotional pains are teaching you. This is not to suggest to go searching for them and digging in your psyche and spending time unnecessarily to try to uncover every single thing that has ever happened to you - because that would be the equivalent of looking for wounds or picking at scars but when there is an emotion that is alive you may act as your mother figure and take care of it.

Taking care of it is not perpetrating it, it is allowing it to heal.

You are always safe to be kind to yourself.

Nothing can slow you.

Kindness should not be something to fear and staying with What-Is is one of the highest and holiest actions you can take.

Time transmutes everything.

There is nothing and no urgency to clear yourself out or change yourself in any way. There is no need for you to be other than what you are because you will find that you are already whatever version you think it is you are trying to become as soon as you accept your Now. It is far easier to begin to act as you want to act and think as you want to think when you stop fighting with yourself. As soon as you accept what you are it is far easier to act in the way that you would like to act and think in the ways you would like to think. Emotions included. You are respecting yourself and the feelings and not asking for them to change. Which are all best practices when any energy appears.

EMOTIONS ARE LEARNT

Emotions, explored further, will reveal themselves to be as fundamental to your existence as your physical vessel. There is a difference between your natural emotional system and the distorted version of it that you learnt as children. That said, each of you has a different temperament. This is not something that is learnt. This is a sensitivity element of your instrument.

This sensitivity is based upon what you call emotions is organic in nature and is perfectly calibrated to aid you upon the journey you are wishing to have. Emotions are misunderstood because they are categorized into positive and negative emotions whereas there are no positive or negative emotions there are simply energies which are delivering different information to you. You have been conditioned, and in fact deliberately taught, which emotions are positive and which emotions are negative. This is arbitrary. It is a system that was created based upon the observation of others as opposed to based upon one's own observation of self.

If emotions were not what you label 'painful' they would not grab your attention in order for you to change course of thought and belief. If it did not hurt when you cut yourself with a knife, how long would it be before you accidentally cut off a finger?

It is interesting to look back into your childhood and remember when you were taught the labels to emotions.

Children do not know that they are sad before they are told that they are sad. They just are. They are in that moment expressing the energy that is coming through them and someone who believes themselves to be more experienced comes to them and says:

"Oh, I can see you're sad."

and the child thinks:

"Oh, this must be what sadness is"

Then the next time they have that feeling, instead of expressing it honestly and letting it go they say: "I am sad." Associating negative thoughts to sadness, they then begin to avoid the emotion in favor of not feeling it at all.

An adult teaches a child what sadness is and in the same moment explains how it needs to be fixed. An adult teaches a child what happiness is when it sees an expression of happiness and in the same moment explains which expressions of happiness are appropriate and which are not appropriate which are acceptable in that specific culture or community which are not acceptable. The being itself does not have these labels. The being simply has the ocean of energies that move through it which left on its own would be the most efficient form of **emotional guidance system**. However, because of the labels and categorization and consequences that we have attached to having feelings it is not as efficient as it would be.

In an ideal scenario a child would be left with its emotions and simply have an adult figure in their life who holds the space for them to have the emotions to last however long the emotions need to last.

You have learnt that the most acceptable way to express emotions is by labeling and verbalizing them instead of simply feeling them.

If you bang your elbow against a wall it will hurt. You do not believe that you can do anything about making it hurt less in that moment or take less time for the pain to pass. In that moment you know it to be a hurt elbow. You know it is hurt because you banged it. Now you will either get yourself some ice, shout to allow the energy to pass or wait, cradling it and stroking it with the other arm. You have learnt not to walk so close to the wall.

For emotions there is a belief that if one labels the emotion it will pass sooner or one can avoid feeling it. In this way the learning that the thought or belief wasn't in service, is delayed and it may take repetitive experiences of the same emotion or circumstance until the lesson begins to be integrated or recognized for what it is.

Emotions are not controllable. They are only suppressed or expressed. They are no more controllable than your bodily functions are. You can hold your urine in your bladder and eventually you will wet your pants. It is the same with emotions. So we are of the mind that in the same way one should not go against their physical nature, one should not go against their emotional nature. Each being is emotionally diverse and will have more or less information from their emotional guidance system at any point in their life. The fact that one needs to be taught this just shows how unfortunate the ideas behind emotions have become in your species. For other animals it is not the case. They run when they are afraid, they cry when they are sad and they dance when they are joyous. We suggest the same for you.

A minute can only last a minute. It is the same minute for any and every experience. It is just that you believe that certain things last longer than others. This is the same with sensation - feeling energy of any sort. Energy just is energy. To place it on a scale and say this energy is worse or better does not take away from the fact that it is inherently energy.

It is you who has added this flavoring to it. This is the condition of the game that you are playing and you have come here specifically to play this game.

When you stop seeing anything at all as a problem as opposed to solving problems, you can now create what has not existed before. Which is why you are here.

There's no suffering and there are no problems. Not all of the drama serves. Although all of it is beautiful and perfect. It serves until it does not.

EMOTIONS ARE NOT SITUATIONAL

Your emotional guidance is never about a situation. Your emotional guidance is always about your perception of the situation. When you have a feeling that does not feel natural to you that is out of alignment with your normal state of being or that feels negative to you, you may always inquire on that feeling: What am I seeing? What am I believing? What am I thinking? How can I think differently?

The emotional guidance system is not intellectual. It does not add stories. It is pointing to beliefs within you that you are ready to let go of.

If someone were to call you an unflattering name and you were to have a negative reaction to that, you would know through that negative reaction that you do not like being called names. It is not because someone is calling you names that you do not like it but because you have a belief that someone calling you a name means something. That is the belief that one can investigate in this way.

When there is a feeling that comes up around a choice it is not the negative feeling about the choice it is a negative feeling showing you that you have a belief that this choice means something.

Clarity is not a requirement for the emotional system to be functional.

Confusion will only bring you more of what you need to learn, or want to learn, and so there is no need to fear it.

While emotions are not controllable, thoughts are. Therefore you do have an indirect access for creating a more harmonious emotional landscape.

Whenever you feel a negative emotion we may suggest adopting your first thought to be one of acceptance of it. This acceptance is always in line with your inner being. Following this thought, we suggest you make small efforts to release and experiment your way into thoughts that feel better than the initial trigger. This may take practice, but eventually you will form the habit of positive increases in your thinking that allow you to learn from your negative emotions at a faster pace.

If you find yourself moving into separate directions emotionally it is an opportunity to refocus your thinking. Mixed desires or energies, emotions or frequencies, exist in order to bring you a move obvious example of the direction you do not want to move in. Then you can become 100% certain of the direction you do want to move in. As there are infinite directions to move in, it is the prerogative of you as a sovereign being to be able to choose within this infinity. It is normal that you are not always completely laser focused. It is normal that you would have some doubt when you have not yet had the experience in the direction that you want to move in. You are tuning your focus and experience and your emotions are tools to help you do so.

While in a healing process it is normal to be hesitant to head too quickly towards your goals for you feel that you are not quite ready. You will never be fully ready for every goal that you will ever have.

The emotional guidance system is very powerful, in this aspect, the moment you feel emotionally bad about something you are giving yourself very clear information about what direction to move in. We would say to tap into your intuition, and your body, more often than your mind, and yet not to vilify your mind, for it is a tool that is often vilified.

Remember that there is no need to have complete clarity. There is no need to get to where your perceive it is that you want to be for where you are now is where you are meant to be. You do not need to put pressure on yourself. You can relax into knowing that even with all the things your believe in yourself to be imperfect you are 100% whole. You are complete. You are perfection. You are an organization of consciousness that has never been here before and will never be here again, it is unique, it is purposeful and consciousness all of consciousness would not be the same without it, it could not exist without it.

You are safe to lean into your sensitive nature and we know that it has been difficult for you, to allow or feel comfortable with some of your more emotive states, but we also want to let you know that many of your emotive states are required because you have chosen to be in service also through that mechanism.

Healing of the world will need to be done through the feeling of the emotions that go with the energetic frequencies and occurrences that have happened. How else would you know that you no longer want to feel this way and make the changes to your thoughts, beliefs and actions that are necessary to that end?

There are these sensitive beings who have taken on the role of feeling the feelings for others who are no longer or not yet capable of feeling their own feelings. It is a gift that they are giving to the collective by being so very sensitive to certain topics for it balances out, those who have become desensitized to them, and it allows them to 'within the collective field' tap into a corrective energy, and a deeper healing, for when one can no longer feel their own feelings, they have shut off the part of themselves that would bring them in the most direct and deliberate way to the end of their own healing process.

BELIEF

If you feel a negative emotion or uncomfortable emotion it is safe to assume that there is a belief behind that emotion. If you were to look at the belief you may still have the **comportment** of the action however you would now also hold the understanding that it is the belief that caused the discomfort and not the circumstance. With this understanding you would know that the aspect required changing is not the circumstance but the belief you hold.

A belief is any thought you have placed your identity into. As your true identity cannot be confined to any container, the moment you hold and identify with a thought and repeat it until you no longer notice that it is simply a thought, you have diverged from your true self and your true nature. Thinking your way up the frequency scale can work with beliefs as well as emotion and thoughts but it may require even more repetition until the new beliefs are fully installed. There is much attachment to beliefs. Just have a look at the games you play on your Internet discussions. All of your worldly strife can be traced back to belief systems, all of them erroneous. However the sense of attachment is a lie, for beliefs like thoughts, are not proprietary. They cannot be yours or define you. Beliefs are interchangeable, casual and relatively arbitrary.

It is unfortunate that you cannot come out of the womb fully formed and instead you arrive with your bodies being so very vulnerable and dependent. In part, this is so that you can develop the connections you and many other species have with community and family group - You are social beings. Although fundamentally it is because your anatomy does not allow for a fully formed human body and brain to pass by the birth canal. This smaller human version does not have the same connections to cognitive thought immediately upon arrival as an adult version does and so must be awarded to a hopefully fully formed adult for its early care. Though many adults are fully formed physically, their emotional mental and spiritual evolution has often been stunted by the time they arrive to care for a new being and so many connections are broken, as infancy, and childhood develops to our realms and other realms to memory. All of the programming that happens on a subconscious level in childhood is then very persistent in adulthood and the cycle continues.

There are two directions[1] for deprogramming:

The first is to endeavor to spend as much time in conscious thought and behavior as possible.

Presently, the majority of adults on your planet have very little time in their day where they are actively practicing conscious thought. Much of the day is on autopilot or lost on thought that is not directly related to being present in the moment. Much consciousness is lost on creativity and though we applaud creativity, it is used in many cases for means that do not serve you, such as worry, guilt, anxiety, fear, speculation or nostalgia. You use the part of your brain that can create in order to create imaginations that have nothing to do with your current moment. To bring back presence and this ability to override subconscious programming one must actually be

---

1 *Used with the meaning: An explicit instruction*

where they are, not in **space-time** but with the experience, observing.

The second direction involves: 1) Adopting the belief that **is** possible to easily reprogram subconscious beliefs. This will make the next steps far easier. It is possible to reprogram anything that they do not desire of their behavior or thinking patterns or relational situations, then they automatically have a step in the right direction. 2) Identify the patterns that are not desirable and replace them with the ones that are. For example, if you have a pattern that says "I am not a naturally happy person" you can say "I am happy" and do as many affirmations as you like, but if you do not know this is the underlying story you are telling yourself it does not matter how many conscious affirmations, visualizations, or beliefs you attempt to apply - they will not succeed. If you can see that the underlying belief is "I am not a happy person naturally" then as your subconscious plays that program you remember the theme tune and as soon as you hear it: "I am not a happy person" you will be able to remember to be conscious and in that moment apply the new pattern. In that moment, you are telling yourself "I am not a happy person", you can tell yourself "I am a happy person." or "I choose to be a happy person. From now on I am a happy person." or similar, for it is hard to override a subconscious program you have been playing for a very long time.

There is truly no benefit in hunting for negative core beliefs because your entire existence is structured in a way to reveal them to you. You can attempt to dig for these patterns but they will present in your day to day experience anyways and the more holistic option is to address them as they arise. You will know you are running this pattern when anything feels difficult, when anything feels bad, because your feelings are talking to you and telling you that there is a belief to be looked at that is not actually true, and if it is not true then it is a pattern that is not serving you.

You do not need to push through. Any negative belief that you are ready to let go of will reappear in the form of circumstance and situation until it is let go of and so there is very little that one needs to do in terms of letting go of beliefs except being aware of them.

If a situation continues to occur one is wise to look into the beliefs behind what is occurring and if they were to change those beliefs would the situation change with the feelings about it change?

So our suggestion would be to relax and watch as circumstances and situations show you moment after moment both what this belief is and how to release it. There is no urgency, in this. You have come into incarnation for in part, this activity. The beliefs that you accumulated that do not serve you are hidden at this moment because it serves you that they are hidden at this moment and they will be revealed at the moment it is necessary and possible for you to dismantle and release them. Until that point, hunting for them and chasing them is possibly distracting you from what's happening in this moment and what can be released in The Now.

You are like an onion, each layer of your skin more and more juicy and closer to the core. But, if you tried to cut into that core without fully peeling the onion. You are simply damaging the bulb.

You can practice patience and self love and know that there is nothing wrong with you and nothing that needs to be resolved. If you are aware of the core belief then it is possible you would benefit from forgiving yourself for having that belief in the first place. You did not choose it and it is safe to allow it to be there. Allow yourself the grace of knowing that it was not your fault to have adopted it.

To have a belief that no longer serves you means that the belief itself served you in the expansion to the point where it was no longer serving. One does well to adopt and create beliefs for oneself to later transcend for if there was no expired belief to transcend then one would remain at the level that one was at.

If you came into the world with only the beliefs of Oneness you would not have very far to go.

The words fault and error relating to any concept is impossible in that all perceived errors are simply perceptions and Creation has no error. Every element including your own beliefs, including all of your perceived faults, in Creation is exactly in place for the motive of allowing you to have the experience of expansion.

Once it is understood that there can never be anything wrong while simultaneously understanding that your desires and personal free-will and perception of imperfection also contains perfection - even if these desires are to perfect what is already perfect there will be a great peace within you.

Once you truly believe that a belief is no longer serving you, you will let it go naturally. There is nothing you have to do except open your hands. If it has not been released yet, no matter how negative it may seem, or how it might impact your existence in a way that is not preferred to you, it is still serving in some way.

Yes, there are those that would tell you to rush and try harder and do more for releasing these beliefs and these are well meaning beings who you have created as permission slips to accelerate but remember that all is as it should be.

There is no prize for assembling the puzzle in the correct order. You may take as much time as you like, for there is no time. How boring it will be when everything is exactly as you think it should be.

You are always connected. Everything until this point has perfectly positioned you to come into your glory. Everything from this point will be seen through the eyes of that glory. From those eyes, all that has come before is also seen as glorious. You are safe to let go of everything that does not serve you. You are accurate in your discernment of your own life and so can rely upon yourself what is right and what is wrong for you. You have the freedom to choose every moment that comes **herefore** in the way that brings you the most joy.

nowing is what is beyond belief. It is the absolute acceptance of what is without cognitive awareness or additions. Knowing is native to you. You **are** knowing.

You do not need to know anything. You are not here to know things but you have access at all times to an energy beyond beliefs that is simple knowing. You are always moving towards what you want. You cannot move in any other direction.

You do not need to know anything because you already do know. To have a need for something implies a lack of it. You do not need anything. Certainly not to know. To align with the What-Is is to align with what you call God, the Universe and Source. You have so many names for it. You spend so much time naming and talking and thinking about it and yet you at any time could step directly into it. And you do. As do we.

Things are far simpler than you are making them out to be. Your mind was never meant to hold all of these discernment and judgments of self and circumstance and other. They are clutter.

Stop searching. You are found.

You do not see the entire picture from your perspective. You cannot see the entire puzzle from the perspective of one piece of the puzzle. You must shift your perspective if you want to see how the puzzle piece fits. And remember you do not need to see how the puzzle piece fits. You just know that it is part of the puzzle. You value it.

You can at any time pull out your point of view and see the entire puzzle or at least see all the pieces and see how they fit together. But the one that is the piece of the puzzle will not see the entire puzzle and so to see the entire puzzle one is no longer a piece of it and must be all of it, or beyond all of it.

We assure you - you fit in. It would not be complete without you. It could not be complete without you. You were created perfectly. The situation and each moment is created perfectly for the big picture. There is no need for you to see the big picture. It's shifting. It shifts as you move and evolve and all those around that connect with you, move and evolve, frame after frame, moment after moment shifting to different timelines choosing different realities. And yet in the one that you choose you are

KNOWING IS NATIVE

always the central piece of the puzzle.

So how can one know? How do you see the big picture?

Decide what it would be for you. If it is the painting of how your civilization becomes enlightened, then paint that painting and know that this is the painting that has been cut with a jigsaw into seven billion and more pieces and watch how they come together to form that painting, image - the one that you chose.

You see the big picture only by painting it yourself. For you cannot be wrong. And if in the picture you are seeing obstacles and contradictions it is because you are painting it. Choose not to paint obstacles and contradiction if you do not want obstacles and contradiction. If you do, then choose to paint it!

The puzzle will always come together anyhow. It always does. It is always whole. The puzzle is whole right now. You are part of the whole puzzle. it is already complete. There is no confusion.

Do not lie to yourself. Do not say that you want something that you do not want because you will get what you want, not what you say that you want. Then you will be confused and you will say "why is this puzzle not coming together the way I said I wanted it?" It is because you do not want it that way.

The puzzle is already together and you are already in place. You are already exactly who, what, where, when you need to be right now - right now reading this. And you are already perfect.

Perfect in the eyes of the Creator - who is you.

There is no position or set of circumstances required to be able to connect with what you truly are. You will, in fact, find that your comfort levels are dependent far more upon how confident and comfortable you are with yourself, than they have to do with the atmosphere, beings, or circumstance that surrounds you.

This statement applies not only to service but to every experience and moment of your existence.

State of being always comes from within and is always only reflected externally. Each time you have a small confirmation externally of what you already know or believe to know you will allow yourself to move more in the direction of that knowing or belief. Please note that as your external circumstances are confirming internal beliefs and you are taking your confirmation from your external circumstances you must be very astute in choosing beliefs that at a fundamental level work with you towards your goals and not away from them. As you can see, there is no inherent discomfort in any situation apart from the discomfort that you add to it.

To transform anything, the first thing to do is: See it as neutral. Because if it is neutral, it needs no transformation.

ntention is your main source of power. If you can consciously choose your intentions you can create reality in front of your own eyes. Of course, with this knowledge we will caution you to choose wisely. All intention setting has its effect. Most of the effect is on you - the one who sets the intention. As you begin to shift your intentions from all others to the one truth - the intention to love, you will find that most of your problems and challenges dissipate and vanish.

Intending will produce what you are intending - but primarily in its energetic form. Whatever you intend is what is coming to pass. If you intend to harm, you are creating harm whether or not you perceive of a physical manifestation of that harm. The harm does not even need to land on the object of your intending to have been created and chosen. Even if you are sending harm because of your blindness to your own intentions, perhaps because you are unaware of your distortions in this direction, the harm is still being created in this time-space reality. It is this reason that we suggest that if you were to focus and be aware of only one thing in this experience it would be the root of your intending.

Harness your ability to see what your intention is with every word and action and then discern if all of those intentions are in alignment with the love that you are. Any action or thought that does not match the high frequency of love will be highlighted by your emotional dissonance with it and then you have the opportunity to realign and choose love instead.. For love is you tapping into yourself, your true nature and will. This love, this giving, this generosity and this willingness is changing you into more of who you truly already are. It allows you to expand your heart, and in expanding your heart, you are expanding the heart of All-That-Is because it is all One.

In the awareness of shifting your intentions to love you may uncover beliefs which no longer serve you. As this occurs you may ask the question 'If I do not intend to love in this moment, what am I intending instead?' Any answer to this question is a vibration that is not in full alignment with who you truly are and you

INTENTION
CREATES REALITY

are safe to readjust in whatever way necessary. This rule also applies to how you treat your own self. If you are not intending love to be the outcome of all of your actions you are intending something other than love and this is what will appear in your experience.

In the end one does not send love to another for the benefit of the other. One sends love to the other because they are that love and because they are choosing to experience themselves as that love. These wise souls know that other is themselves and their intention and the subsequent reality that that generates will be of their preference. We are One.

It could seem very selfish that the only reason one would send love to another is that it is itself, but this is what love is. Love is the recognition that another is oneself. We encourage the setting of love as one's main intention because it is the only intention of the All-That-Is, even if it seems to not be the case. When you are witness to circumstance and experience that does not seem to you to be the vibration of love we encourage you to hold the intention of healing and wholeness yourself. In this intention and this vibration, you will find your own healing and wholeness thus allowing you to see the situation in a clearer fashion while simultaneously dismantling the need for the situation to present in order for you, and all those like you, to reach a space of choosing what would not seem to be love in your experience in order to learn the lessons, yet again, that all of it is.

Expectation Is Not Intention

There are many who teach the holding of positive expectations as a way to manifest more swiftly one's desired outcomes. While this is a useful practice and we always encourage reaching for positive thoughts do not rob yourselves of your personal power of creation. Expecting an outcome is not the same as intending it.

Expectation relies on the external circumstances while intending is all on you. Expectations are not choices, you are not choosing when you are expecting something. You are hoping in a positive direction. Hope comes from the perception that your world can be conditional. You are running a lack belief programming when you hold hope and expectations because if you chose and intended you would Know and your experience would reflect this knowing. An expectation can only exist when there is doubt of your chosen outcome. And if there is doubt in your chosen outcome, then what you will receive is doubt.

This of course means that one cannot get attached to a specific outcome that they are hoping for. If you believe that the highest experience would be the manifestation of a car or a higher paycheck you cannot honestly intend that outcome to come to pass. There will be an aspect of your being that naturally shifts your intention into the lower vibration of hope because what kind of car you have specifically is of complete disinterest to the All-That-Is. Instead, the All-That-Is is fascinated by your potential for love, happiness, alignment... These things can appear with or without your preference of vehicle (and are often impeded directly by your preferences.)

Teachings that remind you to release expectations and preference, do not do so because expectations are bad, but because when one has expectations, they will receive something different than what they expect. This is the teaching nature of experience and contrast. Personal preference does not align with the intention of love for in love one would love whatever did or did not arise in their experience. Holding the expectation and preference points to an opportunity to learn more of this lesson and your higher self loves an opportunity to help you to learn more of what you are wanting to learn.

The next time you would like to peer into the future we would suggest choosing and intending over hoping or expecting.

CHOOSE FAITH OVER DOUBT

There is a game of doubt being played out on a collective level for your civilization because of the increase in catalysts that would have you choose. So, doubt arises to remind you how important it is to choose. Doubt arises to remind you that, without a doubt, you truly can control your entire existence.

The opposite of doubt is faith. That is the beautiful lesson of this sentiment. Doubt will push you, eventually, to choose faith. Faith is created through wise intention.

A wise intention is one that cannot fail to provide. The intention to love or the intention to choose love more often, is a guaranteed success.

It is also wise to leave the future be, and bow in the humility that while you know, you do not Know.

And not knowing, is the purest and wisest choice you can make, because it brings you back to the What-Is and the Self, which is all you could truly ever know.

Intending Action + Goals

The power of any action is only as strong as the power of its intention. There is no action without intention arising first. Any action unbacked by a strong, conscious intention is futile. There is no point in action on its own and it is impossible. The only action without intention is one that you are partaking of without awareness of the intention behind it. There is however always a conscious or unconscious intention to every action.

Intention is what brings any action to fruition. In action backed with conscious intention there is the inability of failure towards the intention.

However, there is always the higher intention and the universe working in your favor to bring you to your learning lesson. Sometimes one cannot trace back outcome to their original intention because they cannot zoom out to a distance wherein they can observe the original intention that put action and then results in motion.

In regards to setting goals, we would say that setting goals for the Now, as opposed to the future, is far more beneficial. If you set your Now goals and intend towards them your long term goals will simply unfold in a surprising way that you could not have predicted. If you set the goal and intend to be in your highest vibration in each subsequent Now, it is impossible that your long term goals will not be achieved all on their own.

Intention and faith are the greatest goal achieving skills that one can practice.

Intention is what puts the building blocks of your reality in front of your eyes in order to be able to be used. Mastering the art of intention, is equal to mastering the art of self assurance, and eliminating elements such as doubt.

Gratitude + the Miracle

When you believe that your intention does indeed create your reality you will be able to create your reality based upon your intention. All you must do is decide what feels good to you, intend for that to be the outcome sensation-wise of whatever it is that does occur, and you will find that, regardless of what transpires this sensation appears in your experience.

This is why gratitude is so powerful. It is the intention to feel good and be grateful for what one has. If one is grateful for what one has one can only have the sensation of being grateful for what one has. Therefore nothing for which one would not be grateful could arrive in one's reality.

If you could tap right now for a moment into the actual vibrational frequency of gratitude, which you can by intending and practicing gratitude, what you will find is that all other frequencies begin to vibrate similarly to it like a tuning fork. Gratitude or appreciation is one of the highest frequencies that a human can achieve and one of the easiest to practice achieving without, for example, an external circumstance to have to stimulate it. It is just a question of aligning your mind with the truth of What-Is because the truth of What-Is is that whatever is a miracle.

Whatever **Is** is a miracle.

The fact that you can experience anything at all, the fact that you exist at all; is a miracle. Remove every question from every mind on your entire planet as this miracle sinks in and becomes All-There-Is. The frequency of All-There-Is is that sense of it being a miracle.

And so when your father is dying of cancer it is a miracle.

When you're watching your child take their first steps it's a miracle.

When you're biting your toenail it's a miracle.

Your teeth - they grow out of your face; that's a miracle.

So gratitude is simply aligning with What-Is. It is recognizing and intending to admit to the miracle. Being grateful for the air going in and out of your lungs is recognizing the miracle of that fact. Being grateful for your neighbor taking your post when you've gone on holiday is a recognition of the miracle of that fact.

Practicing gratitude is the tool that will bring you to the closest interpretation of the truth that there is for your minds to adopt. The rest is the job of the heart and aligning with love.

The practice of gratitude is not commonly a human practice only because it has been conditioned out of you. Fear, or the ability to be controlled allowed you to adopt other beliefs, but a small child knows nothing but the miracle. They know nothing but gratitude. They are a living example of it. Watch a child as they examine a leaf sitting on the surface of a pond. If you slow down and watch you will see the magic of all of existence occurring in your Now.

You can truly enjoy anything with gratitude. And of course, gratitude is a synonym for love.

It is perhaps easy to set very small intentions, as opposed to trying to create from nothing something like 'the intention to live one's calling'. These mini intention to love, moment to moment add up during the course of your days and years until you will find that your calling comes to you, your car or any material goods come to you, the correct relationships and experiences come to you. Your true desires arise based upon the collection of the small desire you have to be more in alignment, to be more love, to be more of who you already are. You are the collection of all of your small desires and the biggest desires within your heart, those ones of being of service, come from the intention to feel good. The specifics don't matter at all. Anything specific is transitory.

Yes intention is extremely powerful. It is very powerful in writing as well as in words. We suggest for you to move with a state of fearlessness. We suggest you tell your intentions to yourself so you can get used to hearing them, and also to hearing the voice within you that negates them. You can start to tell that voice, that you are grateful, that it has been protecting you and that you are ready to experiment with this new direction.

This is how each pixel of your reality gets placed in front of you.

*I*t is not Vagrein's intention that upon understanding the concepts outlined in this book we strive to become something that is extra-human. One major aspect of their teachings has consistently been the embracing of the human experience with all it's nuances. Vagrein does not propose that we become godly, or alien to our true nature, rather they propose that we accept what we originally intended to be as humans in the first place, pre-incarnation.

The following is a written channeling that was offered to a friend of mine on the necessity of fully immersing oneself in the human experience and acceptance of all the aspects of humanity that flow through us.

Upon reaching deep levels of self-realization, one can believe themselves to be beyond the matrix of the more mundane, or seemingly mundane daily existence and experience of circumstance of everyday reality. This is the case, on one level, as the Self is beyond the scope of daily activities. The reality that one can perceive with their physical senses is indeed, not relevant to the true Self which has an exit, a **carte blanche** to exist in perfect harmony beyond the **matrix**. We will not introduce, at this point, a concept of dualism for it is not the intention and not the purest under-standing of what follows. In this belief one may begin to imagine they are beyond being human and we propose that it is only one who very much is human who could, while in their physical incarnation, even begin to imag-ine this concept.

The Self is comprised of many facets. Again, not separate, not dual, but regardless faceted and without which could not connect back into the whole. The daily experience in an incarnation is not to be overlooked in this faceting for it is the ultimate creative expression of the Self that is beyond it.

A being, upon incarnation, which, please understand is also only one aspect of the illusion, creates the experience, and experience of experienc-ing, that is most relevant for the Self - capital S - to experience more expansion than was otherwise and pre-viously or simultaneously possible. It is because of this that each and every expe-rience is valid, is treasured, is necessary, not for the growth, specifically of the

ON 'BEING HUMAN'

individual individuation of consciousness but of the whole.

When circumstances occur in one's life to which one does not have a sense of preference, these experiences have been created to put in play both the experiencing of these experiences, from the optic of having never been before from this direct perspective, and the experience of these circumstances being made available to the individuation in order to trigger further expansion towards a direct realization of the one true reality which is the absorption into the All-That-Is oneness whole integrality of existence.

Where there is an individuation which is in confusion as to the 'why' of multiple non-preferential experiences occurring - with the understanding of the ideal/concept that 'reality' - or at least physical reality as it is experienced, is an illusion, there is the possibility that the individuation is not looking at the causality of their preferences in the first place but, also an invitation to meet the circumstances with the higher perspective of the illusory reality being as valid and as desired by Creation, simply because it exists, as the 'truth' of the fact that all of Creation is illusory.

An embodiment of a self-realisation is not only the sharing and transmission of the knowledge so that other-selves, in the illusion, may have the grace and peace that comes from the letting go of identity towards oneness but also a transcendence of the idea that any hair is out of place on the head of Creation.

A car crash, an injury, a personal tragedy are all invitations to call back, call in the knowing, not only, that the act/event in itself is an illusion but, as there is no aspect of reality, illusion or not, that is not real, it is also an invitation to come into the knowing that while illusory, the circumstance, the relationships and the essence of all-that-is is part of the All-That-Is.

There has been a distortion, due to the nature of conditioning, to imagine that simply because something is true its seeming opposite is false.

The fact, and it is fact, that reality is an illusion does not mean, by default that the illusion is not reality.

Although these ideas seem diametrically opposite, a complete understanding of this concept arises when an individuation surrenders to the illusion as if it were real with the holding of the knowing, not the understanding or thinking, that it is not.

To negate, on an active level any aspect of reality will ultimately lead to examples or opportunities which point towards the inability to negate reality. Reality and illusion are intrinsically linked in both directions.

The experiences that are not of your preference in your experience are here to show you that you are ready, not only to be present with the reality of Self beyond individuation and form, but to be present within form and call in all of the amazing gifts that lie within you and come from your Self-realization.

If you are not allowing yourself to be human in the confront of circumstance because you are feeling that your knowing of Self beyond form should be guiding your incarnation you are putting pressure on a system that was not meant to perform in the way that you ask.

If you are using the mantra of 'It is all an illusion.' to disallow the human parts of the Self beyond form to experience what is naturally being called through this incarnation your reality will provide experiences that will challenge you in an attempting to break this pattern.

Are your reactions to circumstances 'I know better than this' and 'This shouldn't be happening', or are they 'I do not know anything at all' and 'I will allow what is to be what is'?

We ask you to experiment with being human for a while.

Experiment with 'losing your shit' - as the vessel might say.

We ask you to forget everything you think you know about self-realization in order to begin to truly live with self-realization.

The only way to truly transcend the self is to allow the human to be what it is a beautiful and necessary and wanted part of the Self.

You do not need to fear a less-than version of yourself that reacts in a human fashion to circumstance. You do not need to fear losing your state of being or state of well-being, by getting angry when anger appears, getting sad when sadness appears, getting scared when fear appears. You do not need to chase these internal experiences away to maintain your state of self-realization, in fact, you are now being asked to allow them. This does not mean to revert to a version of self that is out of control. It means to acknowledge that the Self is never, ever either in control or out of it. It means to look at the experience and know that it is illusory, but not to negate its impact, value and the human reaction to it. The experience is not an illusion to the human. The human is not separate from the Self, and the Self cannot be lost. The Self is not the one that is trying to maintain self-realization by negating reality. It is only the human who can negate reality. The Self already knows All-That-Is. The Self already knows that all is accepted, including both whatever you cannot accept and the non-acceptance of your inability to accept it. As you confront what appears to be not wanted or what appears to be a challenge moving forward, perhaps you may adopt the new mantra of 'Am I honouring All-That-Is?'. From there you are past the mantra of 'what is - is an illusion'.

Think to yourself: Am I honouring the feelings of the being that is in the illusion responding to this experience in a valid fashion? Am I honouring the experience or circumstances' right, or need to be here? Am I allowing all that can be allowed and where has my knowledge of self-realization limited my ability to allow? Am I honouring the experience and the experiencer or only honouring the witness? As there is no separation between these elements, to dishonour one is to dishonour all and therefore correction in perspective will be requested and the opportunity to correct presented.

There is nothing to solve or work out. Challenges will arise. This stage is subtle. There is no threat up ahead if you do not 'figure this out'. No, you should not know better by now because there is no You to know better.

But that does not mean it is invalid to think that you should know better. Honour this as well by seeing that this is the pattern in this now.

There is the ability to step aside and watch all of the illusion while being smack dab in the middle of it. Both are you. The All-That-Is is you. The human self is you. The human, and all of the human experiences, reactions, confusions, fears and disappointments are the All-That-Is.

Do not fear your emotional body. There is no need to worry that if you were to allow it free reign it would negate all that you know and all that you are. It is only as powerful as you are giving it power. It is beautiful and as significant and insignificant as any other element in All-That-Is.

You are not here to transcend humanity. You are here to create it.

*agrein* discusses many aspects of what is happening in our world and how we can, from a higher state or perception and by accessing the higher states of consciousness that we can all tap into, manage and navigate this and any challenge that comes to greet us as a learning opportunity. Much of this chapter on current events was channeled pre-Covid-19. All of it is as, if not more, relevant since the changes that we have experienced on a global level.

Because they have access to multiple realities and timelines and a general overview of each of our perspectives, Vagrein does not go easily into predictions or prophesies, rather they continually guide us back to our own knowing that it is ultimately each of us, individually that chooses the future for the collective that we are then witness to.

In this chapter they do address some of the more common questions that arose in the lead-up and initial stages of what we are now experiencing and what we can continue to experience. Please ensure that you distill the essence of the answers provided knowing ultimately that you are a sovereign, empowered being.

There is nothing external to you. There is no grand conspiracy to control you via mass-media or the entertainment industry. The current state of your communications resources is as such because you as an individual and a collective have chosen, time and again, complacency over action. As you process messages now arriving in your experience that you imagine to be external do not allow yourself to be lulled further into complacency. The system is as it is currently because there is such a high demand for this form of suicide that it needs to be manifested in accordance to your will. Short term it may seem easier to 'not think' or 'zone out' in front of your televisions, and accept what is being spoon fed to you, but in truth, the price you pay for that habitual choosing is much graver than you think. Allowing yourself to believe in the external and that it has power over you is a surefire way to renounce your own ability to respond in a way that is aligned with your higher calling.

As we talk about what is currently happening in your world we ask you to tap into which of

NAVIGATING CURRENT EVENTS

these issues are most active in you presently. With this in the forefront of your mind, please continue.

As a collective you are slowly waking up to the consequences of your choices. These manifestations or catalyst are a prompt for you to change the way you are choosing your experiences, however many of you are looking at them as another reason to fear making these changes.

If you continue to make the choice to end your growth and development in this incarnation in favor of remaining stagnant, then the only holistic and organic option for you both as an individual and collective is the ending of this incarnational cycle. This is not a warning or due to some force of malevolence in the universe but rather an honouring of the direction that you in your own free will have chosen.

It is not the bad food and the routine and the entertainment that make you sick. It is your choice to stop growing and your choice to stop evolving. This is how the seeming bad food and routine and information match with your vibration and appear in your reality.

If you are choosing to cease your evolution, the universe in its frugal resourcefulness will arrange for you to continue with your soul's journey on another path. Your body will be recycled and your soul will have the opportunity to start again and make new choices. You are so completely free that you are as always, provided with the option to believe that you are in cages, powerless and what you would call doomed if you so see fit.

However, in all the infinite possibilities, you determined this particular experience and incarnation would be the most interesting or fun way to spend what is not Time.

In reality, nothing is truly happening. Your soul is watching a film that includes all of the players and story lines that you believe will be of service to you.

Even if you spend your remaining years sitting under a tree nothing would happen. Even if you start a revolution that changes the world completely nothing would happen. It is all your choice. Nothing that was not meant to happen could happen. Nothing is happening that is not meant to happen. The question is will you choose now to work with and learn from what is currently occurring in your events or do you continue to shun your responsibility deferring to many other-selves, just like you, who also choose to defer theirs?

Your response-ability is for you to align with your higher self and furthermore, to understand that yourself is the Whole and to align with the Whole.

When you see examples of circumstances that do not resonate such as what you call suffering or injustice, you can choose to balance that injustice by whatever means knowing that the injustice that you are seeing exists only for you to have the opportunity to balance it. For if you did not seek that game, it would not be the game you are playing.

It may be hard to understand that this is an illusion.

The things that you label as atrocities are light and shadow dancing on the screen of consciousness. Their pixels arrange in mathematical formation for you to experience events that will trigger your growth in a direction you chose to grow in.

From this perspective, there is no world to be saved, for all one would need to do is rearrange the mathematical algorithm that lights in sequence each of these pixels to display a different image. This is simply done by choosing to do so and accepting no beliefs that do not align with what you would prefer to witness.

This is what you understand as shifting timelines or choosing what you would like to see or raising your frequency. In this way reality transmits a new image which is more in alignment with your new frequency.

You have infinite power as an individual. In fact it is the only space in which you have power... but it is infinite. Simultaneously this is a collective and you are co-creating via shared intention but intention is slippery if not consciously created and there are many who co-create non-deliberately.

So, were you to have a part or responsibility for saving the world, your first and best step would be to understand the mechanics behind what that means.

Take your steps back from interacting directly with physical reality and interact with it at the energetic or mathematical level. Focus on your own energy and maintaining the frequency, beliefs and feeling state that you prefer to experience in the collective. Then you may use your skills and knowledge to continue to inspire those who are creating unconsciously with their addiction to drama and lower vibrational states by teaching them, or expressing to them, the possibility of things being different than how they perceive of them.

Some of you may remember just twenty years ago that your reality was a very different place. Perhaps there was less awareness of some of the events or situations that you know of now. Much has been exposed. However, there was also less understanding of these principles.

The reason why things seem to be getting worse, or are being shown to have been worse, is because of the direct relationship to the change in frequency towards the positive, or, towards the reality of how things work.

As your choice to change becomes more strong within you, what needs changing will bubble to the surface for you to be able to dig your hands into the clay of creation and mold it. At the same time these events arise because you have chosen a reality where you truly want the other-selves you see among you to join in your creative pursuit. What you see as negative events arise as a push to gain hold of those who are creating unconsciously so that they may walk alongside you.

The best way for existence to gain hold of those who create unconsciously is to stimulate fear, sadness and anger until they can tolerate it no longer and choose to embrace their own power instead.

Your responsibility is to eliminate the addiction that you have to these emotions, and to never waver in the stimulus of them.

Your second responsibility would be to share with others how to do this. Thoughts and words change which pixels light up. Think of the pixels you would like to light up. Speak of what you would like to see, and do not think or speak of anything else.

We would now like to talk about a misunderstanding which is currently quite diffuse in the minds of the people of your planet including those who enjoy thinking of themselves as awakened or on the spiritual path. This misunderstanding is proposed to you repeatedly and consistently on a minute by minute basis and is so familiar to you that it has become part of who you believe yourself to be.

We are talking of the idea of good versus evil. As you may imagine from our previous conversations we do not hold in our space of consciousness the concept of evil for we are able to see a broader perspective without judgment of the actions of any and all. We do know however that upon your plane of experiencing there are beings and actions that you are less preferring. There are actions that go against the very fiber of your being. Things that are horrific or that you see as such. We do not discount or disregard that there are strong emotions tied with these circumstances as the emotions are indication of your preference and your desire to choose differently. However, we would like to propose a clarification that the battle, if it were a battle, you are choosing to wage is misdirected. There is not a war of good versus evil. There is instead the choice between oneness and separation.

In any situation that you can look upon and claim to be wrong or evil you will see there is a common underlying thread of separation. There is, likewise a common underlying thread of separation in your reaction to that action and a distancing that takes place as one observes what is not wanted from a position of righteousness or from a position of holding a strong desire for another preference. If this desire is held without an acceptance first of the What-Is and an appreciation for the catalyzing element that the circumstance has brought to you, more separation is generated.

When one is judging anything as evil one is automatically separating oneself from that thing and in doing so adding to the stockpile of separation that created that so called evil in the first place.

If you have within your hearts the will to see good prevail the only arm in your armory is to absorb All-That-Is as oneself. This is the only way to cap the fire of separation. You will be tempted, as information comes into your awareness, and you see what is being revealed to you, to celebrate the misfortune of those who were abusing power or causing harm to other-selves or in a position of inflicting pain. This temptation, to further separate yourself from those whom you would label as evil, is how the darkness, in its very sneaky and ultimately serving way, seduces you back into separation.

We are not saying one should look upon acts that are not of one's preference and celebrate them either. We are not saying that one should support anything that is against one's beliefs or will or abuses the free will of others. What we are saying is that as you are presented with whatever you see as separate from you to remember that it is the fact that you see them as separate that allows that form of separation to continue to exist within all of consciousness. In oneness, which is contagious when practiced and is in truth all there is, all circumstances are resolved.

You are warriors, not cowboys in a rodeo. You have within you the ability to choose a completely different way of seeing the world.

The only reason why there are horrors on your planet is because they too are love. These horrors are required by your own and the group consciousness on the planet, because in this moment there's still the option to choose between love and not love, even though not love is also love. It is a game. The more of you who choose to step into self love and into love for the all, will and do provide both the example and the vibrational resonance for those who come after them to step in the same direction. Your experience with learning to believe and know 100% your worthiness, 100% your beauty, will be an example for all those who are around you, for all those that see you, for all those that come to you for counsel for the rest of your existence. This is your paramount job, this is your highest service, and this is what you can do, which is 100% in your capability and within your grasp.

Imagine any situation that you do not prefer as if it were a mosquito.

As you know, there are people in your world who do not have any interaction with mosquitoes and in their consciousness, mosquitoes have zero significance. In this imagining, you may come to realize that your experience with mosquitoes and the relationship that you have created with them is directly related to your portion of consciousness. Anything directly related to one's portion of consciousness is directly related to a lesson that they would choose to learn for themselves.

The narrator also does not love mosquitoes, and yet made a decision in the past several years to no longer be bitten by them. Her relationship with the consciousness of the mosquitoes existed for her in order to learn that she could choose something that seemed radical and impossible for herself and to have confirmation that the radical and impossible IS possible, once one chooses.

It was an experiment and there was some level of doubt, but the lesson was learnt. She is now no longer as victimized in the summer months where mosquitoes seem to prefer her to others at an outdoor gathering.

Every annoyance or challenge that arrives in your field, even those that seem universal is both universal, and personal, because your portion of All-That-Is has chosen to have that experience in order to expand from it.

When presented with what you call evil or injustice or mosquitoes the lesson may not be to choose to not have mosquito bites, but it may be something completely different. The mosquito or catalyst may be a metaphor for some other aspect in your field of awareness so that you can have a beautiful realization. Or it may motivate you to take inspired action to correct the injustice or to manufacture a new form of insect repellent. We are proposing that you at all times are the governing factor. You can choose. You can step out of the woods.

You may choose at any time what mosquitoes or any other uncomfortable circumstance means to you. If the catalyst seems to prevent you from going on hikes, that is your choice. If they prevents you from sitting around a campfire, that is your choice. If it teaches you that reality is an illusion, that is your choice.

Remember too, that you are the mosquito. It would not exist without you and you could not exist without it.

You can give significance to any and all circumstance. You can call it evil and combat it. You can also realize its true purpose, a motivating factor for you to choose who you would like to be in the face of that catalyst. Do you choose to be a victim to it? Do you choose to be its enemy? Do you choose to live in the dis-empowering frequency of fear? Do you choose to embrace it and allow yourself to be inspired into loving change that it is calling for?

Fear, as some external force, does not exist. It is a choice. It is not powerful on its own. If one is afraid they are choosing to be afraid. It is not something that happens to someone. It is something that you choose and that is okay.

The topic is not important. It does not matter if you are afraid of 5G or clowns, the solution is the same. Find the belief inside of you that makes you think that fear is useful or valid.

What would fearing something ever produce? It does not produce safety, it does not produce action. There are things you would prefer or not prefer in your reality. Fear does not bring the things that you prefer to you. It brings more of what you do not prefer to you. If you are afraid of clowns, it is wise not to go to children's birthday parties but if you are not afraid, then you are free to go to children's birthday parties.

If fear arises over any subject it is your internal guidance pointing you to a misunderstanding or belief that is not serving you. Move towards the cause of the fear until it is seen it is an illusion. Once seen as the illusion, there is an automatic shift into a timeline where the thing that was once feared, is now neutral and no longer a threat. Or, it is removed from one's reality altogether.

We know you want suggestions on how to navigate your reality in subjects such as: 'Shall we fight against the evils of the world?'. Again, there is no evil. It comes back to faith and how much you trust yourself.

The battle is always inside of you. The opposition and arguments that arise when you contemplate these words; bring them all back to love. Reality will transform itself to its new understandings.

In this moment, you are safe. You are reading the words on this page. The belief that you could not be safe, is what is creating an unsafe future moment. We guarantee you that even in what you believe may be an unsafe future moment, you are also safe.

Connecting with your primal fears is only a good thing for as you look at it, it can be released, felt, and let go of. It exists within all of you. It is natural. It is part of your biological makeup but it is keeping you far smaller than you could be otherwise. There's nothing wrong with being afraid. So you can allow that. You can feel it. You can investigate what it's telling you and nothing bad will happen to you by doing so.

An animal runs when they are afraid because they are not holding in that fear. They are not repressing it. They are simply allowing it to be and move them in the way that they feel is necessary. As a human you can feel fear and allow it to move you or you can feel fear, decide that it is being caused by beliefs that are not serving you and you are not actually in danger and that you don't want to run away in that moment. Then you can sit with the fear or you can choose to ignore it and repress it and hide it. It is asking you to look at something. What could be lacking?

See how useless fear really is, and tell the part of you that is afraid that it is okay. And if at all possible, don't watch Stephen King movies[1].

If you're aware of the potential of going towards the light and love or going towards fear and darkness, then you are playing games with yourself. There's no drama. There's no dilemma.

Please keep in mind that there is no alternative to Self, even darkness or pain or shadow or any focus upon that is more growth and is more of Self.

We will confirm that you are currently as a collective dipping in and out of several timelines. There's the one in which you are fearful of the future and the one in which you are neutral about the future.

We reiterate that any timeline that you are in is of your choosing based upon your frequency, what you are focused on, what you are thinking about and what you are feeling about what you are thinking about. We will point to the fact that when something feels bad it feels bad - this is simple. When

---

1 *An example of the entity groups' humour: In reference to the earlier exampl of fear of clowns. I saw the TV show 'IT' based on the Stephen King novel of the same name as a child and carried a fear of clowns for many years.*

something feels good it is closer to the truth than the thing that feels bad because it is closer to your truth and the truth of what you would like to see in the world.

Focusing on anything that brings any form of fear is taking a step away from the timeline that one wants to see develop and since all reality is created based upon the intention of the individual. The intention of the collective in navigated from your individual point of perception.

It is up to the individual to shepherd their own intention so as to be able to shepherd the reality that presents itself to them.

In the case of the future of humanity this leaves you very much with the ball in your court for it is you who gets to decide, based upon how you think of the future and what you want to see, which future will present itself to you.

You can experiment with this. You do not need to believe what we are saying right in this moment. All you would need to do for your experiment would be to focus only on what you would like to see in the world and then see how opportunities and situations present themselves with the solutions that you are already looking for.

There is nothing that is outside of your control, and we are sensitive to the fact that it does not seem this way. In part this is why we choose to talk with you.

There is nothing to fear but fear itself[2] for it is fear that will create the reality that you do not prefer. There are beautiful beings in your reality who know this and whose role it is to catalyze fear within you so that you may wake up from fear by deciding that it is no longer how you would like to feel.

You are safe to let go of any beliefs that are not serving you and adopt those that do.

Any topic exists for several reasons.

The first is that you choose for it to exist, and on a collective level you are choosing for it to exist.

Remove judgment from any topic and one suddenly has to look at why they were judging it in the first place. What is the logic behind judging

---

2 *Often attributed to Roosevelt, Franklin Delano during his 1933 inaugural speech for president of the United States of America*

something?

Climate change, for example, is being judged because one is afraid of death of humanity and the death of the planet. Have you asked yourselves why?

Why attribute the death of humanity and the death of the planet to the climate changing when you are so successful at killing the animals on the planets and killing the vegetation on the planet and killing each other without the climate doing anything at all?

You may focus your energy on worrying and arguing and fearing climate change. You may adopt fear for a circumstance that feels beyond your individual control or you may focus your current behaviors and make choices in each of your moments that cease killing each other and the planet and the animals. You are not truly facing a climate change. You are facing your own choice to not face anything at all.

Remember that when a collective comes to a point of enough discomfort it is necessary for them to change course. There is always the simple road or the difficult road to the same destination. The difficult road to a destination includes feeling very uncomfortable for long enough until one decides to no longer be in a position to create discomfort for themselves.

The comfortable road involves seeing that the discomfort is unnecessary and simply no longer creating the discomfort.

This is a vibrational and frequency based choice. It requires an individual to be diligent about their thoughts, actions, and which beliefs they are going to choose.

Many are the stimulus in your current environment that point towards you choosing fear as opposed to faith. The faith is not required on an external level. You do not have to have faith that everything will be "okay", you just have to have faith in yourself. For the moment that you believe that something needs to be okay you are demonstrating that you do not have faith. Faith means that you do not require external circumstances to match your preference to remain in a high frequency state.

This is a lesson many of you are wanting to learn at this time.

This is why things are presenting themselves in the way that they are.

This is also why half of your population believes that things are getting worse while the other half believes that things are getting better.

They are simply choosing the more difficult or the simpler route.

If you pay attention to where your focus is most of the time, you can begin to understand which route you have been choosing and very quickly moved to the more comfortable route if you prefer.

It is not necessary. Nothing is necessary. Nothing is happening. Nothing is out of place.

The actual sequence of events in your life, including those that seem to be on a collective level is absolutely inconsequential.

Your growth will happen whether that uncomfortable situation resolves to your preference or not and whether or not your planet bursts into a ball of flames.

Never assume that anything is real, unless of course you want to, but if you do want to, know that there will be the effects of the assumption of that thing being real. We sustain that you get to choose what the outcome of every single event that enters your consciousness will be.

You get to choose.

You get to choose if things miraculously get better.

You get to choose if aliens land tomorrow.

You get to choose the invention of a new fruit.

So while we see that there are collective themes that you are playing with, our only advice would be to be a part of the collective that is choosing what you would have happen. Actively choose with faith in that power.

We promise you, you cannot get it wrong. You cannot make a mistake.

Many of you fear choosing a positive outcome for the stories in your heads because you feel as if you would get your hopes up and be proven wrong somehow but remember even in the worst case scenario - which is that you turn out to be a fool - the entire time leading up to the end of the story - you felt good.

There is no benefit for feeling bad until the story turns out well and if you imagine doom and then find salvation well then you have spent your life imagining doom, and what kind of life is that?

As you choose faith you will be directed to action that supports the outcome that you choose through faith.

So back to this example of climate change; you will be directed to actions that support your improving the climate through your desire to improve the climate, not through your fear of a climate in deterioration. You are therefore safe to let go of a fear of not participating in an improvement of the climate.

This applies to every topic if you look at your history. Perusing all of the previously predicted disasters and all of the end of the world scenarios that have been creatively planned and transmitted you would laugh and you would see how ironic it is that when the world did not end you did not celebrate in equal measures to those that you previously feared. Why did you not celebrate on the day that the world did not end?

On this today, any number of unseen and unknown factors could have happened in your reality to destroy life as you know it but in your reality the world did not end today! You did not die today - and yet you are not celebrating.

What we see is a crisis of consciousness believing there is an external crisis, whether it be economic, climate, political, health and so on and in so creating one thereby focusing the collective in this direction at this time. As you know, any direction that one focuses in with intention is the powerful creator of that reality. As you focus your energy collectively in a direction for creation of reality you are creating it.

There is a simple solution considering you are all creating your individual realities within the collective reality. The collective reality can, but does not need to, influence the individual reality. The individual reality does however completely influence the collective reality that you are then witnessing. Each of you who does not wish to have a collective crisis may simply stop choosing to have a this crisis and this will be reflected in their experience. It is a re-frame that if held steadfast truly does have the power of changing your experience.

Choose for yourself when faced with any challenge a solution that seems most feasible to you with your current level of belief, and understanding that this choice will resolve the entire crisis for you.

For example an individual could choose today for all of the nations of world to wake up and decide collectively that something drastically holistic needs to be done about the climate, global economy, world health and wellbeing of all. If that one individual were to choose that with conviction and belief it would be what would occur in front of their eyes. It would be a suitable resolution to a problem that they believed was of a global nature. This being, however, for you to reap the benefits of their intentions, needs to be you.

Another individual who had a different form of belief systems could wake up tomorrow having decided today that there is no crisis and that they need no permissions that need no government to turn around and say that there isn't a crisis or that there is or that they would pledge to resolve it but they could just wake up tomorrow and the scientists, facts and news could have all been wrong.

A third person could make this same decision today and wake up tomorrow and the problem never existed in the first place.

You are that powerful. You get to choose.

The planet that you individually are on is responding to you and your choices as a collective in the same way all of reality is responding to you and your choices.

It is not separate from you. It is part of your body. It seems large and it seems complicated and it seems like it is not within your power but it is. You may need a permission slip and you may need certain events to happen for you to believe that these issues could be resolved, but we assure you that you do not.

If this book is that permission slip and let it be. If not let something else be.

If your desire is to quote-unquote 'save humanity' then you are capable of doing so whether it is through your action or your creation of the action of others or you creating a sequence of events that leads to that resolve.

The only thing you have to know to save humanity and save yourselves is that there is nothing to be saved from and that saving yourself from this nothing takes far less effort than you believe it does.

W e are very cautious when talking about potential or probable futures as it is of our intention to reinforce the knowing within each and every one of you that whatever experience you have in your existence is your choice. This is one of our primary teachings.

There is always the potential for any experience. You specifically focus on the experiences and predictions you focus on for there is some part of you that is excited about and interested in them. This is a path that we do not say you should not honour, in that we are not saying to drop these concepts and we are not saying that these concepts are false, it is your choice which and what of these concepts you would like to take with you.

We do see the people of earth coming to a tipping point, where there will be choices made and the choices will at times reflect more dramatic results. For the choices that are being asked to be made now are choices that are more dramatic because you have placed yourselves in a corner with your indecision. There is both the possibility for a dramatic conclusion to that indecision and a very mild and tame continuation of the indecision or a beautiful, 'my little pony' conclusion,

But we will reiterate that the choice is yours, each of you gets to choose, the unfolding of events. Each of you gets to choose your role in the unfolding of the events.

You exist, you are part of the All-That-Is, it is unnecessary to be anything other than what you are.

It is exciting though.

The illusion of time is compressed into one moment. The past, present, and future of any soul's incarnation are all in the Now. In the Now a soul is deciding its fate and using will to choose its next action, vibration, and timeline. Simultaneously, this incarnate being's fate is already completed. In effect they are also already dead. Their lifetime is already complete. In that lifetime whatever was to occur, occurred. Including all of their roles, all of their relationships, their purpose and anything that they would have ever interacted with. Your entire lifetime is already, in this Now, complete and simultaneously occurring, complete and about to be-

PREPARING FOR THE FUTURE

gin.

From the perspective in which you are choosing to place yourself in as you read this, you are at the midst of a lifetime. You are in the Now. You are choosing moment to moment what will happen next. You are in the driver's seat, the front row. You are in the most exciting point of this story. You're both the audience and the lead character. You're the watcher.

We have called this chapter 'Preparing for the Future' but of course that could never be. There is no accurate prediction of the future because it is you who chooses your future. It is you who controls what we are about to say to you next. All of Creation is a mirror. All of it is a reflection. All of it is your painting. Even that it is cut into nearly 8 billion pieces by the jigsaw is a creation of yours. It is not cut into 8 billion pieces. There is nothing to try to fit together. It all fits together because it is one.

Let go of all of your ideas. Align with What-Is.

Pull back to 'the One that observes'.

By One we do not mean 'individual'. We do not mean One as 'a one' of 'many'. We mean 'The One'. 'The One' not 'of many'.

Pull back to 'The One that observes' and observe without judgment, without ideas and from there you can see the picture and how you do not need to see the picture.

There will be a new wave of interest in spiritual development shortly. Stimulated by catalyst that cannot be ignored. We would advise that those of you who already have established a deep understanding of spirituality via unity and love prepare to embrace the impact of this wave, as the beings that come to your door via this catalyst will be hungry and would not have had as easy a path as you did in their awakening. Alongside these beings, there will be others, who via the same circumstantial experience will lose hope or will completely.

We do understand that you are often fooled by circumstances and forget that circumstances are not entirely real so we would say the best thing to do for the next two years would be to focus on keeping your feet firm if there should be a storm.

Regardless of political events, there is the intention and calling out for change and change involves transmutation and circumstances will have to reflect this request for transmutation.

Know that at the end of every bush-fire, the soil is far more fertile. The match has been lit.

We know that all it would take for everything to be okay, is for you to believe that everything is going to be okay.

While the collective does exist, there are infinite collectives, and the determining factor of the collective is the individual perspective of consciousness of the collective. Much of what we would advise for you in facing the future is outlined in the previous chapter on how to navigate what presents itself currently.

Anything you would like to see occur in your future Now requires the intention of the collective to occur. It is something that will be seen or experienced or perceived on a global level and requires the participation of the free will of the majority of the beings on your planet. However, the free will of that majority of the collective on your planet depends upon the perspective of the one individual perceiving of the free will of the beings on that planet. What this means is that you as an individual have the power to choose what the free will of the other beings on the planet would be. This is because in the infinite realities that are available you get to choose the one that you experience. We know that does not seem to make sense because if they had true free will, then an individual could not choose their free will for them. However, each individual portion of consciousness exists in its own seed, so to speak, where it has a reflection of All-That-Is within its own bubble or seed. Each transparent seed has a nucleus, a cell that is the you that you perceive of as your individuation. None of these cells actually interact however in each cell there is interaction with the elements of the whole. It is up to each cell to decide how they would like to see the whole interacting with them. This is why each individual is so powerful.

It is your free will and intention that determines how you will experience the collective, as you perceive it, going through any circumstance.

You also have the ability to also choose to perceive, for example, your neighbor having your same experience, or not. Perhaps you choose to perceive of your neighbor as having reached the criteria to ascend at this moment so you will watch them from your laser beam heading up to the heavens. You can choose for everyone to ascend simultaneously. You can choose for some to not ascend. You can choose for this not to be your reality at all. There is no absolute reality except the One Reality. Which is, there is no absolute reality.

Do not put too much pressure on oneself to achieve any specific belief upon this or any topic. It is not your responsibility to save or enlighten anyone else as outside of your seed they do not exist. However, you may choose ascension or world peace or enlightenment in the same way as you may choose anything. It is not your responsibility to choose for an other-self because of the way that each cell has its own nucleus, which is governing its existence. You, in your reality have the responsibility to choose what you would see in your reality, and nothing less, nothing more.

Your reality does not affect the actual reality of the other beings because there are infinite parallel realities.

You are able to shift to a version of earth where disclosure or free energy or ascension is imminent or already happening. You may remember too that you are also simultaneously rock matter. For the parallel realities include All, and they simultaneously include all beings that you currently know and do not know. So, if you encounter someone on the street, know that they are also you in a parallel reality. Every animal is you in a parallel reality. Every hair on an animal is you in a parallel reality. It is infinitely possible that infinite things could happen.

You, as virus are presently finding a new host, and this could be equated to the ascension process from the perspective of the virus[1]. You, as a deer, are being eaten by a lion. You as a diamond are being cut into form and set in a ring.

So while yes, you may shift to any reality that you currently know of, know that you are simultaneously shifting to every reality that you are not currently aware of. You are not currently aware of the movie that you are not choosing to witness unfold for yourself. The only thing that gives you a semblance of linearity of your current reality is the fact you choose that you have a semblance of linearity. This choice is not conscious as you speak of consciousness, it is just What-Is.

You choose and you are choosing and there shall be celebration, for what you want is always happening in your timeline.

Things will not stay like this much longer for you. You have been accustomed to your present existence for a long time now. The awakening is accelerating and there are changes on the horizon. For many, it will bring relief for the thought of continuing as you have been is becoming unbearable. For others, it will bring mourning and a sense of loss, but only because you are so used to what you have known.

------

1   *In a transmission prior the the Coronavirus situation*

As you get to choose what these changes are that we suggest that you do not think small, and that you do not think along the lines of what has been built before now, for you are in a space, where you truly can have the reality that you want. Your choice will be made with your intention as well as the thoughts that you are thinking on a daily basis, your beliefs, and your vibration.

We assure you that we see this as a beautiful change and not something to be feared. You are capable and ready, and in the meantime, as you wait and are preparing, we suggest enjoying the reality you are living in now for one day you will look back at these days and you will say, 'remember how it was?'. You will want to have some memories to remember, not that you were distracted or trying to be somewhere else.

There is no urgency, you as a collective have chosen and it's almost here.

Enjoy your suffering, for after the shaking up and settling it is the one thing you will not be able to remember in any form clearly. Enjoy what it has taught you and what it is teaching you. Remember that without it you would not learn the lessons of compassion. Remember that you would not learn the lessons of Oneness. Yes, you are told often that you choose your suffering and you do. You choose it because it is so valuable to you and for your expansion.

Enjoy not knowing. Not knowing is a beautiful thing. If you know everything already you cannot savor the distortion of significance or importance.

Learning. Enjoy learning! Enjoying knowing something you didn't know yesterday. Enjoy that spark of realization where your brain connects something. You may enjoy these things now. It is not to say that they are missed, it is just to say they are not available in Oneness.

You may also guiltlessly enjoy confusion, and misunderstanding, drama. How interesting your lives are with these elements!

These things are only available now, and for as much as you want to criticize them or claim that they are not optimum or not as good as, they are beautiful, absolutely beautiful. You cannot in your full alignment help but to be part of the solution. There is nothing you have to do to be part of the solution except be who you came here to be.

Free will is a bitch.

Of course that is humour, but we say that because the way the game has been set up means that each of you have the option to choose to be other than what you are naturally, essentially, internally, and in doing so have distanced yourself from your own desires. Each of you desires to see joy in the face of a child and each of you desires to feel safe and feel love. In your confusion, and comparisons, and sense of separation you have used your free will to silence these elementary desires and you have introduced fear over the most simple of concepts that is: the Creator created you exactly as you are, for the exact reason that it created you.

Free will allows you to question the Creator! It is in your prerogative to do so and to learn from that questioning, but there is a more straight route to seeing joy in the face of a child and feeling safe and being in a comfortable environment. Thy will be done. Thy kingdom come[2].

You see, the only true will is the Creator's will because any will that you may have has been created with you.

Understand that your will is the Creator's will and the Creator's will is yours and it resolves the worthiness paradox. It resolves the self love paradox. It resolves the love for others paradox and it positions you to be activated to be your highest version! You cannot fight What-Is, because it has already won and the game that you have come here to play really is to simply realize that you are the Creator. So there is nothing left to do but be you.

Your experience is perfect. The Divine Source of All Things chose you to have the experience you are having whatever it may be, including your reluctant hesitance, because it is exactly what it needs to know more of itself at this moment in time.

Learn to appreciate whatever is not what you would like it to be. Learn to understand that this is the will of the Divine All That There Is. This is the will of Source. This is the will of the completion of infinity.

You, exactly as you are, are needed by the completion of infinity for the completion of infinity to exist. You are the missing puzzle piece in the jigsaw of Creation. Even whatever you believe in yourself to be imperfect, is part of that piece of the puzzle. You are exactly, and always will be perfection. You cannot fail at being the one that is needed to complete the story of infinity.

Cultivate your understanding of this one fact, and this is fact, that without you the universe would not exist.

---

4 *Here Vagrein has reversed the original ordering of Matthew 6:10. King James original verse:*
"Thy kingdom come, Thy will be done in earth as it is in heaven."

It would not.

It could not.

Infinity could not exist without you.

The experience of being human is beautiful.

Be You.

This is the only future preparation you will need.

You get to choose.

I n order to write this book I was instructed to awaken every morning at 4:30 am to go sit at the computer and allow Source/Vagrein to come through me with unimpeded flow. The first stages involved organizing all the content that had already come through in the public and private sessions for the reader and later it evolved to include channeled writing sessions during the time I was in front of the PC.

On the day that I began to work on this chapter (today), I closed the computer at the time I would normally begin to help my children get ready for school. I went to their room to cuddle them a little while in the sleepy transition to waking.

As I lay in bed with my daughter, the messages from Vagrein continued to arrive as downloads, as they often do, outside of my normal channeling periods. The concepts of acting, performing and play continued to arise in my consciousness.

She asked me to remind her of the Italian word for acting, which is 'recitazione', She must have been tuning into the same energy.

I thought of the etymology of the word... to re-cite; to quote again what has already been offered. I thought about how acting is the repeating of the original words of the screenwriter or play-write and thought nothing more of it.

The day continued.

After dropping her at school, while walking back towards my home, my vision suddenly changed. This was welcome as I had been listening to and practicing the workbook from 'A Course in Miracles[1]' where one has to repeat over and over 'I am determined to see things differently.'

I didn't know it would be literal.

The people I passed on the street, saw in their cars, and riding their bicycles, had suddenly all become the three year old versions of themselves. It was like walking through a giant kindergarten where in every corner there are children blissfully engrossed in their games. The construction workers who were taking selfies on the bridge over DaVinci's Naviglio canal were children playing with their friendship, connection and new technology in the beauty of their environment. The woman sitting on the park bench with her dog was a toddler wondering at the miracle of her puppy. The mother and child walking were playmates sharing a moment of make-

---

1 "scribed2 by Helen Schucman, A Course in Miracles
(1976 (New York: Viking: The Foundation for Inner Peace),
2007 (The Foundation for Inner Peace, 3rd ed.))

EPILOGUE

believe in which they had decided earlier, before the game, which roles they would play: 'This time you be the mommy and I'll be the big kid.' I could see how in other games and moments of play, they had agreed to play the roles in reverse.

No one I saw was who they are or what they were doing. They were all children of Source, children of God, pretending to be in the role that they were acting in and pretending to perform the actions associated with that role.

The vision changed again.

Now the children were not even their own direct younger versions. I no longer saw their gender, what they were wearing, their race or physical configuration. Now they were light beings without form.

The beggar on the corner was light pretending to be a beggar. The woman with the crutch was light pretending to have had an incident that hurt her leg. The dog on the leash wasn't a dog anymore. Now it was light, attached to light, still a child of God, pretending to hold that configuration.

There was, and still is, a smile completely plastered onto my face and tears running down my cheeks.

The light being that I am was making believe it had a smile on its face and tears running down its cheeks. I could see the game that it was playing. The experience it was choosing to have and the script that it was re-citing in the moment.

But deeper... the feeling itself, the emotions and sensations of complete love, holding and bliss that was running through the system provoking the physical reactions and expressions were themselves light pretending to be a feeling of complete love, light and bliss. It too was a make-believe occurrence in the All-That-Is.

Separation finally vanished. The hack, or cheat code was installed and the computer game revealed. The matrix was penetrated. The veil was lifted and the knowing of Vagrein/Source's messages on a visceral level replaced it.

The leaves are a child of Oneness pretending to be leaves. The lamppost is a child of Oneness playing dress-up. Everything is not only interconnected but is actually the same thing.

All-That-Is is so beautifully innocent - just playing.

The realization has opened the knowing that every form of judgment I could ever hold is foolish. How can one judge a small child for simply playing? How can I judge these light beings for wanting to experience what it would like to be a superhero and attach their cape to their shoulders or a villain who robs the bank? How could I even judge the child who wants to pretend to be judgmental for a moment?

I had heard talk of bliss, Samadhi, seeing through the veil and an integration of Oneness before but as they said earlier, I had not actually chosen to change the game of make believe that I was engaged in, and as soon as I put down those accessories, props and toys in favor of playing this new game of this understanding it suddenly arrived.

*I will admit that I had as much doubt as any of you. I made-believe that I was skeptical and my levels of faith in the possibility of full transformation were shaky at the best of time, but the intention and will was always there. The **desire** to truly know these states and experiences and live my life from this place were fundamental in my script, but as Vagrein shared in the first part of this book: "You will know that All-is-One." a splinter of me imagined they were talking to someone else, and that this book was for someone else.*

I see now how that could never be.

All is One - This is the What-Is

As you walk down the street today, see if you can play this game... See everyone you meet as a three year old child immersed in their own imaginary play.

The baker is not really baking, she is only pretending to. The man on the motorcycle is not really speeding through the traffic light, he is only pretending to. The mother and child walking hand in hand are not mother and child, they are the same age, innocence and authority. Today they decided to be mother and child. Tomorrow they may play again with the roles reversed. See how beautifully innocent they all are. See how dedicated they are to making the game as realistic as possible. See how engaged and focused each one of them is and how they get every detail of the characters they are inventing down perfectly. Just like children, if you try to tell them it's just a game, they will stamp their feet and tell you you're wrong (or pretend to) and so they should - through play is how they grow.

Now look at yourself. You too are just pretending to read these words.

You too are pretending to be a man or a woman. You are pretending to be in the mood you're in. You arranged it all before you started the game. In reality, you're a perfectly innocent little being, just wanting to experience the world.

It is my deepest honour and joy to have been able to play the role of the segment through which this book chose to flow.

It is my deepest wish that it has brought you one step closer to an understanding of Oneness and the beautiful benefits this understanding brings.

May you be happy, may you be healthy and most of all, may you be free.

# GLOSSARY

A

abundance
Having what you need when you need it.

All-There-Is / All-That-Is
Literally all of existence. Also used in reverent context and can be substituted with concepts such as God, Source, the Creator etc.

arts, the
Also called fine arts, modes of expression that use skill or imagination in the creation of aesthetic objects, environments, or experiences that can be shared with others.

allopathic medicine
Science-based, modern medicine.

augur
To foretell or give promise of. Used by Vagrein as a confident wish or blessing.

awareness watching awareness
Meditation/contemplation practice used in non-dual and self-inquiry lines of spirituality.

B

Bashar
Multidimensional being who speaks through channel Darryl Anka.

belief
Any thought you have identified with.

belief systems
Interconnected systems of beliefs that one has identified with.

bliss
State of alignment with All-That-Is.

C

carte blanche
Full discretionary power.

catalyst
Substance that enables a chemical reaction to proceed at a usually faster rate or under different conditions (as at a lower temperature) than otherwise possible. A situation that provokes or speeds significant change or action.

Cayce, Edgar
(18 March 1877 – 3 January 1945)

was an American clairvoyant who claimed, uniquely, to channel his own higher self.

channeling

The act of allowing source energy to pass through one's being without the interference of mind.

channeling state

Trance-like state of consciousness achieved by quieting the mind, renouncing ownership of one's body and mind and allowing what seems to be external consciousness to flow through.

Christ, Jesus

(c. 4 BC – c. AD 30/33), also referred to as Jesus of Nazareth or Jesus Christ, was a first-century Jewish preacher and religious leader. He is the central figure of Christianity. Most Christians believe he is the incarnation of God the Son and the awaited Messiah (the Christ) prophesied in the Old Testament.

Creator, the

Term used to signify the intelligent energy used behind all of Creation. Can be substituted with concepts such as God, Source, All-That-Is etc.

co-creation

Several perspectives uniting in intention and reality presenting the amalgamation of the collection of these intentions.

collective

Denoting a number of persons or things considered as one group or whole.

collective consciousness

Consciousness that is shared by a collective of individuals.

comportment

Personal bearing or conduct; demeanor; behaviour.

consciousness

The energy powering All-That-Is

D

density/densities

Conceptual levels of consciousness, consciousness dissected to be more easily understood by the human mind

desire

Motivating factor for action

distortion

Any concept or belief that does not hold unity as its focus. Any concept of belief that prevents a clear view of All-That-Is

E

ego

Synonymous with 'Separation' and can be described as any form of separation in its myriad of forms.

emotional guidance system

System outlining the function of human emotions in one's life journey

emoto-physical body

The container that includes emotions and physical mater and their interactions

energetic

Consciousness in pre-physical form

enlightenment

The permanent state of self-realization

entity

Any being, individual or group that hold a specific frequency range thereby able to be identified as a unit or distinct faction of the whole.

etheric realms/ether

The 'matter' or energetic container of all pre-physical materialized existence.

extrasensory

Any sensation ability that is not connected to the typically understood sense organs. Some examples are claircognizance, clairvoyance, mind reading et cetera.

eye-gazing

The practice of deliberate sustained eye-contact with another being.

G

generosity

The act of generating more wealth for all

grounding

Centering one's soul in their body, and in turn, connecting it with Earth or the reality of All-That-Is.

H

hallux

The innermost digit (such as the big toe) of a hind or lower limb.

herefore

From the Middle English hēr-for; equivalent to here + for. For this: instead or in consideration of this, with a view to this. Obsolete except for in Scotland.

Hicks, Abraham

Group of entities that are "interpreted" by Esther Hicks. Abraham has described themselves as "a group consciousness from the non-physical dimension".

Hicks, Esther

Esther Hicks (née Weaver, born March 5, 1948), is an American inspirational speaker and author. She "interprets" the entity group Abraham Hicks.

higher-self

an eternal, omnipotent, conscious, and intelligent being, who is one's real self.

I

incarnation
The act of inhabiting a physical body for a lifetime

intention
Deliberate life force energy applied to action

intuition
A sense of knowing not obtained via typical sense organs.
isness

What is

L

love
The recognition of another as oneself.

lucid dream
A dream in which the dreamer is able to deliberately influence the circumstances of the dream or maintain full awareness of the fact that they are dreaming.

M

MacGyver, Angus
Fictional secret agent character armed with remarkable scientific resourcefulness to solve almost any problem using mundane materials at hand. The character was depicted in the 1985-1992 television series of the same name.

matrix, the
Mathematical framework defining physical reality

multi-dimensional
The various layers of a given subject, topic, experience reality et cetera.

O

other-selves
The self in another version, seemingly separate with physical, mental or emotional delineations. Another person.

P

parallel existence/reality
Any one of infinite alternatives to what one is current aware of.

past life
Tuning into a parallel reality which has relevance in your current experience that seems to have come from a past incarnation.

permission slip
Any seeming external tool, situation, entity or experience which one uses as a catalyst or excuse for significant acceleration and growth.

populus

From Old Latin (since mid-2nd c. BC), from earlier poplus, from even earlier poplos (attested already since early 5th c. BC[1]), from Proto-Italic *poplos ("army"), further origin unknown; perhaps from Etruscan or from the root of pleō.

R

reincarnation

The seeming reconnection of one's individuation with a new physical vessel.

resistance

any idea or action that is not in full acceptance of the What-Is

S

Samadhi

A state of deep concentration resulting in union with or absorption into ultimate reality.

sane

From the Latin sanus "sound, healthy"

scintillate

To throw off as a spark or as sparkling flashes.

self-realization

Realization of the self before personality, body, belief, thought and language. Realization of the witness.

simultaneous realities

See parallel reality
somatic
of the body, physical

soul-stream

Continuous flow of higher-self through and to an individuation

Source Energy

Energy that unimpeded by mind flows from the All-That-Is

space-time

Also called space-time continuum. The commonly experienced four-dimensional continuum, having three navigable spatial coordinates (x, y & z) and one temporal coordinate (now). The physical reality that exists within this four-dimensional continuum.

synarchic

"Joint rule" or "harmonious rule". Beyond this general definition, both synarchism and synarchy have been used to denote rule by a secret elite in Vichy France, Italy, China, Hong Kong and Mexico.

T

time-space

This four-dimensional contin-

uum has three navigable temporal coordinates (past, present and
future) and one spatial coordinate
(the non-local Self). Experienced
when one is able to pierce the veil
of space-time.

U

unconditional love
The absorption of other as self
without seeing or judgment.

V

veil, the
The mental membrane between
knowing All -is-One and the
seeming experience of a separate
incarnated self of individuation
vibration
Frequency with which energy
waves oscillate resulting in there
attracting and forming certain
patterns.

More about JP Herman + Vagrein

Jessica Herman is a mother, life-coach, channel, artist and energy healer in Milan, Italy. She had been on 'the spiritual' path for 8 years when she began channeling for Vagrein.

Vagrein is a non-physical entity group for unspecified time and location who has contacted humanity with teachings of love and wisdom in support of our evolution as a species towards Unity Consciousness.

Contact Us

We would love to keep in touch and answer any of your questions. Feel free to contact us:

Email: vagreingroup@gmail.com

Website: www.jpherman.com

Made in United States
Orlando, FL
25 November 2023

39450829R00113